P9-CRP-478

The Way to Spell

Sacramento Christian College

THE WAY TO SPELL

A Guide for the Hesitant Speller

WILLIAM D. DRAKE · *Associate Professor of Linguistics* · STATE UNIVERSITY OF NEW YORK AT OSWEGO

CHANDLER PUBLISHING COMPANY

An Intext Publisher · Scranton, Pennsylvania 18515

International Standard Book No. 0–8102–0085–6
Copyright © 1967 by Chandler Publishing Company
Library of Congress Catalog Card No. 67–18507
Printed in the United States of America

428.1
D76

·◦⸂ Contents

Bacher + Taylor

1 SB

21 Jan 71

37960

PART II. Word-Endings

PART III. Variations in Vowels and Consonants

PART IV. Downright Irregularities and Further Ways to Avoid Misspelling

⋅₀ᴄ To the Hesitant Speller

The Way to Spell is based on the practical and proven fact that an understanding of our spelling system is the critical key which makes the difference between a good and a poor speller.

If you were not fortunate enough to master our spelling system when you were a small child, you can still make up for it simply and easily by following the steps contained in this book.

The Way to Spell offers you the foundation of every good speller's skill, presented on an easy-to-understand adult level. No matter how poor a speller you have been in the past, you can with this knowledge master with proficiency and assurance spelling problems which have heretofore made you hesitant and uncertain.

This book provides you with the basic understanding of *why* words are spelled as they are. Such information has in the past been accessible only in teachers' manuals or elementary primers. Now it is made available to everyone who wants to learn to spell correctly with understanding and confidence.

You will progress step by step from the simple, basic facts of spelling to the problems which present the greatest difficulties to the hesitant, unsure speller. But these problems will come last, and you will be well ready for them.

There are no gimmicks in this book, no lists of hard-to-spell words to memorize. You will learn instead the right spelling habits. Above all, you need never again avoid using a word because you are unsure of how to spell it.

Whether we are willing to accept it or not, it is an incontrovertible fact that today correct spelling is more than ever required on all business and professional levels, and that poor spelling is responsible for intelligent students getting low grades, for potentially excellent workers failing to obtain good jobs or advancement, and for writers enduring the embarrassment of suspected illiteracy.

By studying this book seriously, you can convert such a handicap into a skill of which you will be justly proud. This is no idle promise, for the method of this book has been irrevocably proved in practice to work with people of all ages, in high school, college, and the business and professional world. Teachers as well as students have learned a basic insight into our spelling system through the use of this book. Read it step by step with ordinary concentration; don't skip around until you have first absorbed the whole picture. Then you can go back to restudy any section you need to.

The Way to Spell is designed to be complete—a systematic guide, filled with concentrated information. And after it has been used for learning, it should remain a valuable reference book.

The Way to Spell

PART I

How Regular Words Are Spelled

Spelling is just a way of putting spoken words down on paper. A word is spelled from left to right in the same order the sounds are pronounced, just as the words on this page are printed from left to right in the same order you would speak them. Any word that is written can be read aloud.

Even though our spelling system is noted for irregularities, the truth is that 90 percent or more of all our words are spelled according to a regular system. If you have trouble with spelling, it is almost certain that you do not know enough about the way regular words are spelled. Learn this way first. It is covered in the first part of this book. Then you will find that the exceptions are not as difficult as you thought, and will be far easier to remember.

1· **VOWELS AND CONSONANTS:** the two kinds of sounds and the letters that spell them

If you were asked what a vowel is, you would probably answer, "*a, e, i, o,* and *u.*" But merely naming five letters of the alphabet does not explain why these sounds are different from the others, the consonants.

Vowels are all "open" sounds; your mouth stays open as you say them. Because it is open, a vowel sound can be prolonged as long as you have any breath. A singer can hold a note on the word *free* until she needs to take another breath, because the *e* is a vowel—an open sound. But if she sang the word *freed,* she would have to stop with the sound of the *d.* *d* is a consonant. It closes off the air and forces the vowel to end.

Consonants are the "closed" sounds: your tongue, lips, or teeth come together and either completely stop the flow of air or cause friction that blocks it. The sound of *z,* for example, in the word *freeze* doesn't shut off the air entirely, but it does bring a stop to the vowel that went before it, just as *d* did in the word *freed.*

Vowels and consonants alternate with each other in endless combinations. There are probably a million words in the English language. No one could memorize individually the spelling of all of them. Yet our spelling system makes it possible for you to learn how to spell most of them, even the ones you have never heard of before.

2· CONSONANTS: the easiest sounds to spell

A group of consonants all by themselves, without any vowel sounds, is unpronounceable, because all the sounds are closed. You can't pronounce anything with your mouth closed. Try saying *"bmtpn,"* for example. These letters cannot possibly be pronounced as a word unless you insert open sounds between some of the letters. If you think you can successfully pronounce this combination of consonants, it is only because you put the sound "uh" (as in *bum*) in between some of the letters. This insertion adds an open sound which is not represented in the spelling.

Consonants offer the least difficulty in spelling, for we have plenty of letters in our alphabet with which to spell them.

3· VOWELS: the key to learning our spelling system

In contrast to the consonants, we have only five letters—*a, e, i, o, u*—to spell more than a dozen different vowel sounds used in speaking. This scarcity of vowel-letters is the main reason why our spelling seems complicated. These five letters obviously cannot always stand for the same sounds. Learning to spell correctly is, to a great extent, simply learning how to spell the vowel sounds systematically.

4· LONG AND SHORT VOWELS

The vowels are called "short" when pronounced as in these words:

fat	a
Ed	e
is	i
not	o
up	u

Now try pronouncing the short vowel sounds all by themselves, leaving off the consonants:

a	e	i	o	u
(fat)	(Ed)	(is)	(not)	(up)

Remember this sentence—"Fat Ed is not up"—and you will always remember the pronunciation of short vowels.

The long vowels are pronounced the same as their names:

a	e	i	o	u
fate	eve	bite	note	cute

Come back to these examples as often as necessary, until you can recognize instantly the sound of short and long vowels.

NOTE: The terms "long" and "short" have nothing to do with the length of the sounds. They are only terms used to name the two different kinds of sounds.

FOR PRACTICE: Read the following words aloud and determine whether the vowel sound is short or long:

brave	rose
skim	ham
fret	bug
box	fuse
hive	scene

Correct answers are on page 57 at the end of Part I.

5· THE WAY TO SPELL SHORT VOWELS

Look again at the words with short vowels above, and notice two things:

The vowel sound is always spelled with a single letter—*a, e, i, o,* or *u.*

It is followed immediately by a consonant, and nothing more.

Read aloud the following nonsense words, all of which have short vowels. The key words are printed alongside to help you remember the short vowel sounds:

(*fat*)	dag	bez	(*Ed*)
(*Ed*)	sen	gub	(*up*)
(*is*)	rin	san	(*fat*)
(*not*)	pon	tid	(*is*)
(*up*)	nug	dob	(*not*)

These nonsense words are like hundreds of simple words you already know, such as **job, pen, rug, man, tin,** which are formed on this same principle. All have short vowels followed by a consonant.

FOR PRACTICE: Pronounce aloud the following words, using *short vowel sounds only.* Read aloud each column from top to bottom. Then read each row across from left to right.

ab	eb	ib	ob	ub
ad	ed	id	od	ud
ag	eg	ig	og	ug

am	em	im	om	um
an	en	in	on	un
ap	ep	ip	op	up
at	et	it	ot	ut
ax	ex	ix	ox	ux

Now place the consonant *m* at the front of each one of the above words: *"mab," "mad," "mag," "mam,"* and so forth. Then try it again, using *d* instead of *m*: *"dab," "dad," "dag," "dam,"* and so forth. Do this with each of the five lists. Repeat the exercise until you can do it quickly and easily.

6· SYLLABLES

The short words listed above are all one-syllable words because each has only one single vowel sound in it. A syllable consists of one vowel sound together with whatever consonants go with it, both before and after the vowel. The word *in* is a one-syllable word. So are the words *pin, grin,* and *drink,* because they all have only one vowel, even though the number of consonants varies. The word *upon* has two syllables: *up·on.* The word *inspecting* has three: *in·spect·ing.*

Words are not just collections of letters placed in a row to be memorized. They are built out of syllables, with a vowel in each syllable. Therefore we begin by learning to spell single syllables. As soon as you know how to spell separate syllables, you will have no trouble seeing how they are combined in longer words.

The first and most common spelling principle you have learned is:

A consonant placed immediately after a single vowel-letter ends the syllable, closes it, and causes the vowel to be short:

fat
Ed
is
not
up

There are about 1,200 one-syllable words in English spelled according to this pattern. There are also hundreds of thousands of words with more than one syllable, which contain at least one syllable spelled according to this pattern.

FOR ADDITIONAL PRACTICE: Have someone dictate to you the following lists of nonsense syllables as you write them. Don't try to memorize them in advance. Spell them by ear.

dag	seb	reg
lib	lom	bod
gan	hig	dat
rud	mup	fon

7· THE FIRST WAY TO SPELL LONG VOWELS

Review what the long vowel sounds are:

a	e	i	o	u
f*a*te	*e*ve	b*i*te	n*o*te	c*u*te

Now read aloud the following words, first the one on the left and then the one opposite it on the right. Notice how the adding of a final *e* changes the vowel from short to long:

SHORT	LONG
bit	bite
cut	cute
fat	fate
kit	kite
mat	mate
not	note
pet	Pete

This final *e* is the so-called "silent" *e*. When added to a short syllable that ends *in a single consonant,* it changes the vowel from short to long. Notice that there must be *only one final consonant* for this change to happen· Here are some pairs of words which illustrate how this principle works:

SHORT	LONG	SHORT	LONG
bid	bide	prim	prime
cap	cape	rid	ride
cub	cube	rob	robe
dam	dame	shad	shade
grip	gripe	sham	shame
jib	jibe	slim	slime
man	mane	spin	spine
pal	pale	Tom	tome

Each pair of words has the same consonants and the same vowel-letter in the middle. It is the final *e*—which itself is not pronounced—that changes the vowel from short to long.

Short vowels, then, can be changed to long ones by adding a final silent *e* after a single consonant.

Ten percent of all the syllables in our language, in both one-syllable and longer words, are spelled according to this pattern.

8· CONSONANT CLUSTERS

So far we have spelled only simple words ending or beginning with a single consonant, such as **man, pet,** or **win.** And we have seen how a final *e* changes the short vowel to a long one: **mane, Pete, wine.** Often, however, two or even three consonants come together in a group, as they do in words like **print, gland, stops, clasp.**

pr nt
gl nd
st ps
cl sp

These clusters of consonants never offer you a problem in spelling as long as you write the individual consonants in the exact order in which they are pronounced.

For example, **clasp** and **claps** are entirely different words, because the *s* and *p* are not in the same order. Reversing the letters changes the word from one pronunciation and meaning to another pronunciation and another meaning. An oversight in spelling may cause you to write a word you didn't intend, or a meaningless word, like *"calsp."* Don't reverse letters.

Pronounce aloud the following words, all of which have commonly occurring clusters of consonants either at the beginning or the end, or in some cases, both. All of them have short vowels:

task	brand	skin	fists	frisk
blend	lamp	clan	trust	crab
grasp	twins	drift	stand	plant
mint	act	flit	swim	

Now pronounce aloud the following nonsense words, which have the very same consonant clusters, but different short vowels:

tisk	brend	skun	fests	frask
blund	lemp	clen	trast	crub
gresp	twuns	dreft	stend	plent
mant	ict	flut	swem	

Have someone dictate this list to you as you write the words. Spell them by ear—not by sight memorizing. Don't go on until you can do this exercise accurately.

Have you noticed that the words in the above list are all short, closed, one-syllable words, like the ones in Section 7? Whenever a consonant, or a cluster of consonants, follows a single vowel, it causes that vowel sound to be short:

an	ant
pan	pants
plan	plants

But here is something new: If *two* consonants follow that short vowel, a final *e* will not make it long. It will remain short. *"Flut"* can be turned into **flute,** because only a single *t* follows the **u.** **Grip** can be turned into **gripe** and **plan** into **plane** in the same way. But adding *e* to **plant** or to **drift** will not change the short vowel at all. *"Plante"* and *"drifte"* would still be pronounced as if the **e** weren't there. Two consonants block a short vowel completely and prevent a silent **e** from changing it to a long one.

Now test your ability to distinguish consonant clusters quickly, even when they look somewhat alike at first glance, by reading the following pairs of words. Each pair has the same letters, only in a different order:

burnt	brunt	slit	silt
mart	tram	star	rats
silver	sliver	swarm	warms

Two points you have just learned:

When consonants come in clusters of two or more, be careful to spell them in the order in which they are pronounced, and don't leave any consonants out.

When *two* consonants follow a short vowel, they prevent the vowel from being changed to a long one by a silent **e.** The vowel remains short.

9· CONSONANT-LETTERS THAT AREN'T ALWAYS PRONOUNCED THE SAME OR THAT DUPLICATE OTHERS: c, g, q, and x

c IIIIIIIIIIIIIIIIIIIIIIIIIIIIIIIIIIIIIIIIIIIIIIIIIIIIIIIIIIIIIIIIIII

The letter **c** has two pronunciations: "s," as in *city;* and "k," as in *candy.* It has no pronunciation entirely its own. We could, in fact, eliminate **c** from our alphabet, replacing it with **k** and **s,** except that we are so used to seeing it and using it to spell these sounds. It would look strange to see *fact* with a **k:** *"fakt,"* or *succeed* with a **k** and an **s:** *"sukseed."*

Fortunately, an easy rule governs the use of **c** in spelling:

c is pronounced "s" only when followed immediately by **e** or **i.**
c is pronounced "k" everywhere else.

Read the following words aloud, noticing how regularly the letter **c** is used in spelling. The pronunciation is printed just above each **c:**

k	k	k k	k
scarf	cop	cucumber	cramp

s	k	s	k
cistern	topic	center	act

Pronounce the following words aloud. Some are real words, some are nonsense:

cab	cob	cept	cill
ceb	cub	cib	crib

g IIIIIIIIIIIIIIIIIIIIIIIIIIIIIIIIIIIIIIIIIIIIIIIIIIIIIIIIIIIIIIII

The letter *g* has two sounds also. The first is the so-called "hard" *g*—as in *gun* and *bag*. The other, the "soft" *g*—as in *gem* and *stage*—is pronounced the same as the letter *j*.

Soft *g*, like soft *c*, occurs only before the vowels *e* and *i*:

gelatin	agitate
gentle	ginger

When a word ends in the soft *g* sound, *-ge* is always used to spell it:

bilge	privilege
college	refuge
huge	sage
large	urge

Why can't these words end in a single *g*?—because *g* is not soft unless followed by *e* or *i*. If the word ended in a single *g*, it would have a hard sound, like *rag*, *big*, or *lug*. Since we never end a word with the letter *j*, we are forced to use *-ge*.

Hard *g* comes before *a, o,* and *u*:

gasoline	golf	gust

and also before consonants:

grim	glad

and alone at the end of words:

fig	flag

So far, *g* follows the same rules as the letter *c*. But *g* has one important difference: an *e* or an *i* doesn't always make the *g* soft.

begin	get	giggle
gear	gift	girl

A *g* will never be soft except before an *e* or an *i*, but will not be soft before every *e* or *i*. However, this problem is not serious. Most words with a hard *g* in that position are simple words you already know, like the ones above.

q ||||||||||||||||||||||||||||||||||||||||||||||||||||||||

q always occurs in combination with the letter *u*, and is pronounced "kw":

quake	queen	quotation
"kwake"	"kween"	"kwotation"

x ||||||||||||||||||||||||||||||||||||||||||||||||||||||||

Like *q*, *x* is also an unnecessary letter. It is pronounced "ks":

box	fix
"boks"	"fiks"

FOR PRACTICE: Have someone dictate the following list of words as you write them. Some are nonsense words, some are real; but all are regular:

scap	helter-skelter	jag	gam
skib	scum	huge	quib
civic	gender	jop	lex

10· ADDING c, g, AND q TO OUR SYSTEM OF LONG AND SHORT VOWELS

c has a "k" sound in the following nonsense syllables ending in *c*, because it is not followed by either *i* or *e*:

fac	rac	ric
mic	lac	

Add the final *e* to make the vowel long:

face   race   rice

mice   lace

Notice how the *c* shifts from a "k" sound to an "s" sound, because of the final *e*. The final *e* does two things at once: it shifts the vowel sound from short to long, and the *c* from "k" to "s."

Do the same with these words ending in a hard *g*:

rag   rage

sag   sage

wag   wage

The hard *g* shifts to a soft *g*, because *-ge* at the end of a word always has the soft sound. Here, the final *e* again does two things at once: it shifts both the sound of the vowel and of the *g*.

Remember that *qu* is pronounced "kw." Thus the letter *u* after *q* is pronounced like a consonant rather than a vowel. *qu* is therefore another consonant cluster, just as if it were spelled *kw*. In the word *quit* (pronounced "kwit"), there is only one vowel —a short *i*. Add a final silent *e*, and the *i* becomes long: *quite* ("kwite").

The regular pronunciation of *c* as "s" before *e* and *i*, and as "k" everywhere else, will help you remember the spelling of longer and more difficult words. For example, the word *fascinate* brings the letters *s* and *c* together. If you sometimes doubt which comes first, remember that if the *c* came before the *s*, it would have to be pronounced "k": "faksinate." This pronunciation, of course, would be wrong. Keep the *c* immediately before the *i*: *fascinate*.

In the word *facsimile*, the letters *s* and *c* also come together. But here, the *c* is supposed to be pronounced "k." Therefore the *s* must follow *c* and come before the *i*.

In words with a double *c*, the same regularity applies. In the following words the *cc* has the pronunciation "ks" because the second *c* is followed by an *i* or *e*:

accident

occiput

succeed

In these next words, however, the *cc* is pronounced like "kk" because *c* is *not* followed by *i* or *e*:

> accurate
> occasion
> occur

The word **secede** (meaning "to withdraw," as the South did from the Union during the Civil War) sounds enough like the word *succeed* to make people sometimes hesitant about spelling it with one *c* or two. But you know now that it cannot be spelled with two *c*'s. If it were, the *cc* would have to be pronounced "ks," just like the *cc* in *succeed*.

11· CONSONANT DIGRAPHS: single sounds written with two letters

As you have seen, our alphabet has a few unnecessary consonant letters and a few more that invade each other's territory. But it also completely lacks several consonant letters for sounds that are used in speaking. Our spelling system has to get around this deficiency by using existing letters to take the place of missing ones. Two letters are combined to represent a single sound:

> th   ch   sh   ng
> thin   chin   shin   ring

th in the word **thin** does not represent a combination of the sounds of *t* and *h* at all. *th* is not two sounds in a cluster, but only one, which is made by putting the tip of the tongue between the teeth. Lacking a letter in our alphabet for this sound, we arbitrarily use *th* instead.

If you break *ch, sh,* and *ng* into separate letters, you will find the same thing true. They are not combinations of two sounds, but single sounds written with two letters, simply because we have no single letters for them. They are called "digraphs," which is a technical way of saying "written with two letters."

In the word **gashouse,** *s* and *h* are two separate sounds. In the word **gash,** they spell the single sound "sh."

FOR PRACTICE: Read aloud the following words. Some of them have a digraph for a single sound (*th, ch, sh,* or *ng*). Some of them have the same two letters but the letters are pronounced separately. Pick out the digraphs. (If a word is unfamiliar, look it up in a dictionary.)

hanging	goshawk
hothouse	richest
bother	vanguard
washing	anthill

For correct answers, see page 57.

12· ADDING ENDINGS TO WORDS

By adding special endings to words, we can change or extend their meaning. The verb *walk,* for example, also takes the forms *walked* and *walking.* We added the endings *-ed* or *-ing.*

The basic word is called a "root" word. The endings fastened onto it are called "suffixes." Suffixes are detachable endings that can be freely placed onto any number of words. The word *detachable,* for example, has the suffix *-able;* so do the words *supportable, breakable, drinkable.* The suffix *-able* means "capable of." Added to these root words, it creates new words meaning capable of being detached, or supported, or broken, or drunk. Let us see what happens in spelling when we add suffixes to our basic system of long and short vowels.

13· SUFFIXES THAT BEGIN WITH A VOWEL

REVIEW: Our short-vowel one-syllable words end in a consonant:

bat	rag	din

If the words end in only one consonant, a final silent *e* makes the vowels long:

bate	rage	dine

Add the ending *-ed* to these same one-syllable words, just as we added it to the verb *walk* in the example above. We get

bated raged dined

Again the short vowel turns long just as it did when we added a single silent *e* and got *bate, rage,* and *dine.* A suffix beginning with a vowel, added to a short syllable, will lengthen the short vowel—just as a silent *e* does—when it is followed by a single consonant.

How, then, can we keep the vowel short when adding a suffix beginning with a vowel?—simply by doubling the consonant:

bat rag din
batted ragged dinned

Remember that when *two* consonants follow a single vowel, the vowel stays short even when a final *e* is added. Any time we wish to keep the short sound of a vowel, we double the consonant that follows it.

> The dog *wagged* its tail.
> The nation *waged* war.
>
> The family *dined* at seven.
> Loud bells *dinned* in the air.
>
> The sun is *shining.*
> The boy is *shinning* up the tree-trunk.
>
> The family ate *dinner* at seven.
> *Dinner* is now being served in the *diner.*

When adding a suffix beginning with a vowel (like *-ed* or *-ing*) to a word that ends in a silent *e,* notice that we drop the *e* and allow the vowel of the suffix to take its place: *shine, shining.* The final *e* was there only to make the vowel long. Another vowel in the same place can do the same thing, and it does not have to be an *e.* If the suffix begins with a vowel—any vowel—the final *e* is no longer necessary, and therefore is dropped.

Let us take another pair of root words—*rat* and *rate*—and apply this knowledge. A dog that catches rats would be called a *ratter.* A man who *rates* the cost of something would be called a **rater.** The dog out hunting would be **ratting.** The **rater** at work would be **rating.** A doubled consonant keeps the vowel sound short, preventing a spelling that does not convey the right pronunciation or meaning. A **rater** wouldn't like to be called a **ratter.**

A word often listed as one of the hundred most frequently misspelled words is **writing.** The error usually made is to spell it with two *t*'s: *"writting."* You know now that this error can be very easily avoided. **Writing** has a long *i* sound. The *t* cannot be doubled, or the *i* will become short. *"Writting"* would rhyme with *fitting.* **Writing** rhymes with *biting.*

NOTE: Even though the consonant digraphs spell a single sound, they are not doubled in any way at the ends of words as single consonants are doubled when suffixes are added:

wish	wished	ring	ringing
myth	mythical	rich	richest

Adding a suffix is even simpler if the root word already ends in two consonants. There is no reason to double, since the two consonants will keep the vowel sound short:

buzz	buzzing	lift	lifted
fast	fastest	print	printable
hand	handy	start	starter

FOR PRACTICE: Add *-ing* to each of the following:

debate	spit	tell	excite
blast	shine	rove	win

Add *-able* to the following:

debate	detest
like	use

Add *-est* to the following:

sad	rare
white	bland
thin	

For correct answers, see page 57.

14· SUFFIXES THAT BEGIN WITH A CONSONANT

Some common suffixes, such as *-less, -ment, -ness,* and *-ly,* begin with consonants. They can simply be added to any root word without changing its spelling. Since they do not place a vowel after the last letter of the root word, they cannot affect the pronunciation of either a long or short vowel in the root. Only a vowel at the beginning of a suffix can cause that change in sound. Here are some examples with short vowels in the root word:

spot	encamp	sad	bad
spotless	encampment	sadness	badly

The consonant of the suffix immediately follows the consonant of the root word, bringing two consonants together. This combination allows the vowel to remain short. Nothing has to be doubled; nothing is dropped.

When a root word has a *long* vowel, the suffix still is added without changing anything:

blame	pave	huge	like
blameless	pavement	hugeness	likely

The final *e* is not dropped. It must be retained in order to keep the vowel sound long. If you dropped the *e,* two consonants would come together, making the vowel short. For example, if you dropped the *e* from **blame** when adding *-less,* you would get "*blamless.*" There is no such thing as "*blam.*"

Another group of often misspelled words is easy to spell when you know this regular principle:

live	lively	like	likely	lone	lonely
	livelihood		likeness		loneliness
	liveliness		likelihood		

In every case, keep the *e* in the root word in order to preserve the long vowel: *live, like, lone.*

Do the same with these additional common words that are often misspelled:

extreme	extremely	sincere	sincerely
hope	hopeless	use	useful
nine	ninety	use	useless
safe	safety		

If the suffix, then, begins with a consonant, simply add it to any root word without changing anything. Even if the suffix begins with the same consonant-letter with which the root word ends, neither letter is dropped—both remain. For example:

cool	coolly	real	really
green	greenness	thin	thinness
final	finally	total	totally

At first glance, it may look as if the final consonants were doubled to preserve a short vowel. However, the doubling is simply the accidental combination of two letters which happen to be the same.

15· c AND g AGAIN

Many words, we learned earlier, end in **-ce** and **-ge,** pronounced with the soft sounds "s" and "j" respectively. When adding suffixes to such words, we must be careful to preserve those soft sounds. If the suffix happens to begin with **e** or **i,** there is no problem, for the soft sound will be retained:

face	facing
huge	hugest
notice	noticing

But if the suffix begins with *any other letter* than **e** or **i,** the soft sound will be turned to a hard one unless we do something to prevent the change. For example, if we didn't make some adjustment, **notice** would become *"noticable"* (pronounced "notikable"). We solve this problem by keeping the final **e:**

change	changeable
courage	courageous
notice	noticeable

peace	peaceable
service	serviceable

Keeping the *e* in this case is not done to preserve a long vowel, but to preserve a soft consonant sound in *c* or *g*.

Similarly, a hard sound in the root word may have to be kept when a suffix is added. Simply adding *-ing* to the word **picnic** would produce *"picnicing"* (pronounced "picnising"). This change is avoided by adding *k* to keep the *c* hard: **picnicking.**

frolic	frolicking
picnic	picnicker

Some words ending in a hard *c* are allowed to shift to a soft sound when suffixes beginning with *e* or *i* are added. Therefore *k* is not added:

critic	criticize	critical
physic	physicist	physical
public	publicity	

16· THE SECOND WAY TO SPELL LONG VOWELS: vowel digraphs

Before beginning this section, review for a moment what you have already learned about long and short vowels:

A vowel is short when the single vowel-letter is followed by a consonant:

mat

It is made long by following that consonant with a silent *e:*

mate

It can be kept short by doubling the consonant:

matter

It is short before any two consonants, whether a vowel follows or not:

mask
masking

This system is completely regular, and it takes care of an enormous number of spellings.

A second way to spell the long vowels has developed alongside this one. This system uses vowel digraphs, or two vowel-letters, to spell a single long vowel sound:

a	e	i	o	u	AND oo
pain	beat	pie	boat	cue	coo
pay	green		grow	few	moo
vein			toe		fruit
they					true

These vowel digraphs are not just used at random. They also fit into their own regular place in our spelling system. Let us take them one at a time:

ai ||||||||||||||||||||||||||||||||||||||||||||||||||||||||||

aid	waif	bail	claim	brain	bait
laid		fail	maim	gain	trait
paid		hail		grain	
raid		mail		main	
		pail		pain	
		rail		sprain	
		tail		stain	
		wail		strain	

These words all have closed syllables. *ai* never comes at the end of a word. It is always followed by a consonant.

ay ||||||||||||||||||||||||||||||||||||||||||||||||||||||||||

bay	hay	ray
day	jay	relay
decay	lay	say
display	may	stray
gray	pray	way

These words all have open syllables at the end. *ai* and *ay* neatly divide up the territory between them. *ay* is used only at the end of a word for a long open syllable. *ai* is used only within a closed syllable.

ei and **ey** |||||||||||||||||||||||||||||||||||||||||||||||||||||||||

eight	veil	convey	prey
rein	vein	obey	they

The digraphs *ei* and *ey* are less common than *ai* and *ay* for the long *a* sound. But notice that they have the same kind of pattern: *ei*, like *ai*, is used only in closed syllables; *ey*, like *ay*, is used only in open syllables at the end of a word.

ee |||||||||||||||||||||||||||||||||||||||||||||||||||||||||

beef	queen	agree
creep	seem	bee
feel	steel	free
meek	weed	see

ea |||||||||||||||||||||||||||||||||||||||||||||||||||||||||

bead	leap	flea
beak	meal	sea
east	mean	
heat	stream	
leaf		

ee and *ea* are used in both closed and open syllables. There is no rule for remembering which to use. Long *e* spellings must be memorized.

Long *e* is almost always spelled with a digraph when it is at the end of a word. For example, *agree, fee, sea, flea.* In a few cases, however, a single *e* is used for the long *e* sound:

be	aborigine
me	recipe
we	simile

ie |||||||||||||||||||||||||||||||||||||||||||||||||||||||||

die	pie
lie	tie

This digraph for the long *i* sound is used only at the end of a few one-syllable words.

oe ||||||||||||||||||||||||||||||||||||||||||||||||||||||||||||

doe	Joe
foe	toe
hoe	woe

This digraph for long *o* also occurs only at the end of words— usually words of one syllable.

ow ||||||||||||||||||||||||||||||||||||||||||||||||||||||||||||

blow	bowl	arrow
crow	growth	borrow
grow	own	follow
low	thrown	shadow
throw		tomorrow

ow follows a pattern similar to **oe**. It is used generally at the end of words and is found more frequently in one-syllable words.

oa ||||||||||||||||||||||||||||||||||||||||||||||||||||||||||||

croak	groan	roam
float	load	roast
goal	loaf	soap

The digraphs **oe** and **ow** for long *o* are mostly limited to final open syllables. In closed syllables, the digraph for a long *o* is usually **oa.** And like some of the other digraphs, it occurs only in one-syllable root words.

Long *o* at the end of words is occasionally spelled with a single *o* rather than with a digraph:

banjo	hello
buffalo	radio
embryo	tomato

Long u and Long oo ||||||||||||||||||||||||||||||||||||||||||||||||||||||||

At this point, you must learn to distinguish between two long vowel sounds that are very much alike: *u* and *oo*. The only difference is that long *u* has a "y" sound at the beginning of it: it is pronounced "yoo." The long *oo* does not have the "y" sound. Pronounce these pairs of words aloud:

coo	cue
coot	cute
moo	mew
moot	mute

ew and ue ||||||||||||||||||||||||||||||||||||||||||||||||||||||||

These digraphs can spell the long *u* sound:

few	argue
hew	hue
mew	rescue
pew	statue

They can also spell the long *oo* sound:

blew	blue
brew	clue
chew	construe
grew	glue

ui ||||||||||||||||||||||||||||||||||||||||||||||||||||||||

This digraph almost always spells the long *oo* sound:

cruise
fruit
juice
recruit

ew and *ue* are used at the ends of open syllables, *ui* in the middle of closed syllables.

oo ||||||||||||||||||||||||||||||||||||||||||||||||||||||||

This digraph is never used for long *u.* It is used for the long *oo* sound and can come either in the middle or at the end of words:

broom   shampoo
drool   too
food   woo
rooster   zoo
scoop
spoon

17· SUMMARY OF LONG-VOWEL SPELLINGS

Long vowels are spelled in two ways: with a final silent *e* after a consonant, as in the word *lane*; or with a vowel digraph, as in the word *gain.*

Vowel digraphs are found almost entirely in one-syllable words or in words that have been built up from an original one-syllable root word:

pay   pain
paymaster   painless
repayment   painstaking

or in final syllables:

approach   repeat
contain   retail
entertain   reveal
prevail

You have seen there is enough regularity in English spelling that a great many words can simply be spelled by ear. In only a few cases did consonant-letters overlap each other so you had to remember which letter to use in individual words. These consonants were *s* and *c, g* and *j.* Just to show you how little trouble it really is to remember which letter to use when you are faced with such a choice, look at the following pairs of words:

sity   city   Gimmy   Jimmy
notise   notice   jenuine   genuine
asid   acid   gerk   jerk
sertain   certain   pajes   pages

In each pair, the word on the left-hand side is misspelled. It probably looked wrong to you immediately, just as the word on the right-hand side looked right. You instantly recognized by sight the correct letter because you had already memorized it from having often seen the words in print.

Whenever you have a choice of more than one way to spell a long vowel, you will also have to remember which is the right way. But this memorizing is far easier than having to remember every single word in the English language letter by letter. Your choices will always be quite limited. For example, in spelling the word *load*, you have only two possible ways: *load* and *lode*. A *load* is something you carry; a *lode* is a deposit of ore in the earth. Both words sound exactly alike. Our spelling system offers two ways to spell the same syllable—but only two ways. The only place where spelling requires sight memory is where more than one way is available to spell same-sounding syllables.

For example, the words *mere* and *prepare* are sometimes mistakenly spelled with vowel digraphs. You have to learn that in these words the long vowel is spelled with an *r* plus silent *e.*

The following pairs of words have long vowels that sound alike but can be spelled in two ways. Each spelling has a different meaning:

gait	gate	roam	Rome
hear	here	sail	sale
loan	lone	see	sea
main	mane	steal	steel
meat	meet	tow	toe

Now test yourself. In the following pairs of words, *only one* word is right; the other is wrong, even though it sounds the same. Pick the one which is right in each pair:

blame	blaim	groe	grow
feel	feal	relate	relait
grete	greet	fruit	frute

Since these are all familiar words, you doubtless had no trouble recognizing the correct ones: *blame, feel, greet, grow, relate,* and *fruit.*

The following pairs also have one right and one wrong word. Again, choose the right one. This time, the wrong one has a vowel digraph in a place where it never is used:

paynt	paint	pray	prai
blow	bloa	blui	blue

This exercise was easy: *paint, blow, pray,* and *blue* are correct. You immediately knew the others looked wrong. The reason they looked wrong is that **ay** and **ue** are used only at the end of an open syllable, not in the middle of a closed one. **ai** and **ui** are used only inside a closed syllable, not in an open one at the end of a word.

18· SHORT oo

Short **oo** is one of the few short vowels spelled with a digraph:

book	stood
foot	took
good	wood
look	wool

Just like the long **oo** sound, short **oo** is also spelled sometimes with the letter **u**:

bullet	pull
bush	push
full	put

IMPORTANT: A short-vowel digraph follows the same spelling pattern as a long-vowel digraph. The consonant is not doubled before a suffix even though the vowel sound is short:

look	looking
wood	wooded
wool	woolen

Consonants are doubled only when they follow a *single* vowel-letter representing a short sound.

19· SPECIAL VOWEL SOUNDS: au and aw, oi and oy, ou and ow

A few vowel sounds are not classifiable as either long or short vowels. They are written with two letters, like the long-vowel digraphs:

au	*aw*
cause	crawl
faucet	lawn
fault	lawyer
haul	paw
sausage	saw

oi	*oy*
boil	boy
coil	destroy
hoist	employ
join	loyal
moisture	oyster

ou	*ow*
house	brown
loud	cow
mound	crowd
pound	howl
shout	town

In each of the three groups above, the digraphs in the left-hand column—*au, oi, ou*—are used only in the middle of a syllable, never in an open syllable at the end. The ones in the right-hand column are used in both middle and end positions.

You have already seen that *ow* is also used to spell a long *o*. This use explains why the word *bow* has two pronunciations and two meanings. When *bow* rhymes with *low*, it means the kind of bow with which you can shoot an arrow, or a knot tied with loops. When *bow* rhymes with *cow*, it designates the forward part of a ship, or the motion of bending the body.

(The digraph *ou* is also used in several irregular spellings, which are given in Part III.)

IMPORTANT: Like the other vowel digraphs, these which represent special sounds require NO doubling of the consonant before a suffix:

boil	boiling
loud	louder
shout	shouting

Consonants are not doubled following a vowel digraph.

20· FURTHER HELP IN SPELLING VOWELS CORRECTLY

Two vowel-letters do not always form a digraph when they come together. Sometimes they fall into two separate syllables and are pronounced separately.

For example, in words like **cooperate** and **reeducate,** two of the same vowels have come together accidentally. There is a syllable division between the vowels:

co · operate   re · educate

A digraph, on the other hand, spells one single sound:

LONG *oo*   LONG *e*

loop   feet

You will come across other words in which two vowel-letters come together but do not form a digraph, even though some digraphs are spelled with those same letters. Pronunciation will always be your guide. The following are some examples of such vowel combinations:

DIGRAPHS		SEPARATE SYLLABLES	
ai	pain	a-i	archaic	ar·cha·ic
	tail		laity	la·i·ty
ea	sea	e-a	area	ar·e·a
	repeal		cereal	cer·e·al
	fear		nuclear	nu·cle·ar
	seat		create	cre·ate

DIGRAPHS		SEPARATE SYLLABLES	
ei	seize	e-i	reinforce	re·in·force
	weird		deity	de·i·ty
			atheist	a·the·ist
ie	relief	i-e	diet	di·et
	believe		client	cli·ent
	fiend		alien	a·li·en
oe	toe	o-e	poet	po·et
oi	foil	o-i	heroic	he·ro·ic
ue	cue	u-e	duet	du·et
	argued		fluent	flu·ent
ui	fruit	u-i	ruin	ru·in
	suit		fluid	flu·id

A second point: Sometimes two vowel-letters come together in the reverse order of a common digraph. These vowels also are pronounced as two separate sounds. Be careful not to reverse the order of the letters in spelling and create a digraph by mistake. Below in the left-hand columns are familiar digraphs; on the right are words with the same vowel-letters but in reverse order:

ai	Spain	i-a	trial	giant
	dairy		diary	diagonal
	detail		bias	guardian
	trait		piano	material
au	haul	u-a	usual	
	fraud		truant	
	exhaust		punctual	
oa	goat	a-o	chaotic	
oe	foe	e-o	neon	geography
	tomatoes		stereo	theory
	goes		peony	
oi	coin	i-o	riot	inferior
	poison		violent	violet
	toilet		lion	

ou	sound outside	u-o	duo
ui	suitable	i-u	triumphant radium diurnal

Now test yourself by spelling the following pairs of words. First pronounce them carefully, noting the correct order of the vowel-letters. Then have someone read them to you while you write them:

daily	causal	dairy	poem
dial	casual	diary	peony
quite	loin	coast	taunt
quiet	lion	chaos	truant

21·THE LETTER y

The only letter which can be either a vowel or a consonant is **y**. As a vowel, however, it merely duplicates the sound of the letter **i**:

SHORT	LONG
Egypt	cycle
mystery	deny
myth	sky
system	type

Only a few words use **y** as a short **i**. Can you add any to the short -**i** list above?

Whenever a long open **i** sound comes at the end of a word, **y** rather than **i** is always used. We wouldn't think of spelling **why** as "*whi*," or **rely** as "*reli*." Only a few words of foreign origin— **alumni, alibi, alkali,** and **rabbi**—end in long open **i**, spelled with the letter **i**. **Alumni** and **alibi** are Latin; **alkali** is Arabic; and **rabbi** is Hebrew.

y often appears as an unstressed ending also, in words like **party, candy, dainty.** It sounds something like a cross between a long *e* and a short *i*. We always use **y** to spell this sound, not *i*. But again, a few foreign words are an exception: *spaghetti* and *macaroni*, for example. Can you think of any other Italian words now being used in English which also end in *i*?

Since **y** as a vowel is identical in pronunciation with the letter *i*, it also causes the letter *c* to be pronounced "s" whenever *c* comes just before it:

cycle   lacy   cyst

When used as a consonant, **y** is pronounced as in the words *year*, *yoke*, and *yard*.

22· TEST ON LONG VOWELS AND SPECIAL VOWEL SOUNDS

Take time out now to test yourself on the vowel spellings you have just studied. First pronounce the following words aloud; then have someone dictate them to you as you write them.

As you can see, the words fall together in groups that have similar spelling patterns. When you can spell all the words correctly, have someone test you again by reading the words in scrambled order, skipping from one group to another rather than giving you all of one group at a time.

bane	scene	smile	denote
slate	serene	twice	before
shame	canteen	incline	forecast
brain	agree	hireling	roasted
detain	ease	likeness	roadster
bray	reveal	type	woe
portray	peace	enzyme	bungalow
survey	peaceable	untie	growth
disobey	peacemaker	try	bowl
skein	recipe	alibi	embryo
mule	rude	claw	haul
vestibule	truce	lawn	fault

huge	taboo	scrawl	pause
execute	harpoon	lawyer	faucet
perfume	moody	awkward	nautical
unused	misconstrue	awning	tarpaulin
argue	chewed		
statue	shrewd		
curfew	bruise		
pewter	recruit		

endow	spout	employ	coin
frown	mouth	boyhood	exploit
scowl	aloud	royal	devoid
powder	county	oyster	ointment
browse	pronounce	voyage	moisture
vowel	scoundrel		

bookcase	myth	reply	dainty
woolen	gym	deny	nicely
understood	system	alkali	panicky
fullest	cylinder		faculty
	crypt		confetti
	bicycle		

23· SPELLING LONGER WORDS

Up to this point you have been dealing almost entirely with simple root words. These words are the heart of your vocabulary. You have learned how to spell their short and long vowel sounds correctly and how to add suffixes.

Now turn to longer words for a moment and see how syllables are put together. The first example is:

introduce in·tro·duce

The first syllable, *in-,* follows the regular pattern of short-vowel syllables. A single consonant closes the syllable, making it short. The last syllable, *-duce,* is also regular, with a final silent *e* making the vowel long.

Now look at the middle syllable, *-tro-*. This is a long-vowel syllable, but it is not a root word, like ***throw*** or ***toe.*** It is simply a long open syllable in the middle of a word. Therefore it is not spelled with a digraph.

The reason ***paymaster*** is spelled with a digraph is that ***pay*** is an independent word which has been combined with ***master.***

Here are other examples of long vowels in first or middle syllables:

acrobat	ac·ro·bat
December	De·cem·ber
frequent	fre·quent
grocer	gro·cer
influenza	in·flu·en·za
locate	lo·cate
October	Oc·to·ber
relinquish	re·lin·quish
secret	se·cret
spider	spi·der
trifocal	tri·fo·cal
united	u·ni·ted
vacation	va·ca·tion

24· VOWELS BEFORE r

All the short vowels have a special pronunciation before the letter *r.* This results in only one spelling problem: *er, ir,* and ***ur*** sound exactly alike. You will have to remember which vowel-letter to use in each individual spelling:

er	*ir*	*ur*
certain	bird	curtain
fern	circus	curve
her	fir	fur
matter	sir	occur
servant	stir	purpose
verb	virtue	pursue

ar	*or*
car	adorn
far	for
farm	ford
market	nor
starry	normal
yard	torture

These vowels before **r** also have long-vowel sounds and spellings, which are more regular:

er	*ir*	*ur*
here	desire	cure
interfere	entire	curious
mere	fire	insurance
period	siren	jury
severe	virus	pure
sphere		security

EXCEPTION: were

ar	*or*
bare	before
care	explore
compare	glory
malaria	more
parent	store
rarity	wore

EXCEPTION: are

Since **or** and **ore** sound alike, you will have to pay attention to that final **e** whenever it occurs. The other long and short vowels before **r** are easy to distinguish:

car	her	fir	cur
care	here	fire	cure

Wor- is usually pronounced "wer":

word	worry
work	worse
world	worship
worm	worth

Normal short vowel sounds are found in some *er* and *ir* words:

berry	peril	miracle
cherry	perish	mirror
errand	there	spirit
herring	very	lyric
merit	where	pyramid

Watch out for reversals in spelling. Be sure the *r* comes in the right place. Read these pairs of words aloud, noting whether the *r* comes before or after the vowel:

warp	partner	purpose	burnt
wrap	practice	propose	brunt
perverted	perspective	girl	affirm
prevented	prospective	grill	Africa
hundred	perspire	perjury	curds
hungered	prescribe	prejudice	crude
fervent	repercussion	pertain	
frequent	representation	pretend	

Pay close attention to these first syllables which are often pronounced alike, with the *r* slurred over or put in where it doesn't belong:

surprise	sur·prise	suppress	sup·press
surround	sur·round	suppose	sup·pose

25· THE ACCENTING, OR STRESSING, OF SYLLABLES

In every word you speak one syllable is accented, or stressed, more heavily than the others. Stressing is such a natural habit of pronunciation that many people are not even aware how strongly they do it. It is often taken for granted that everyone knows all about stress, just because he uses it. This is like saying everyone knows all about the workings of his heart, just because his heart beats. The truth is, most of us don't recognize stress in pronunciation until it is pointed out.

The heavy stressing of one syllable in every word has had a very powerful effect on our spelling system. Learning to recognize stress when you hear it can help you surprisingly in correct spelling.

> FOR PRACTICE: Read aloud the following words in the left-hand column, all of which are taken from the two paragraphs you have just read above. Then look at the printing of the same words at the right. The stressed syllables are printed in capital letters.

habit	HAB·it
aware	a·WARE
taken	TA·ken
granted	GRANT·ed
saying	SAY·ing
about	a·BOUT
stressing	STRESS·ing
below	be·LOW

If you did not place a stress on the syllable where everyone expects it, you would produce a very strange-sounding word. Try saying "haBIT" instead of "HABit," or "BElow" instead of "beLOW." You may even find it very difficult to make this switch for you have always thought of these words with the stress on one certain syllable and no other. The stress, more than anything else, makes a word sound right.

In two-syllable words, such as those listed just above, it is clear that one syllable is stressed very heavily and the other not at all. In longer words of three or more syllables, it is natural to have a second stress in addition to the main one. Multiple stress is a matter of rhythm, just as heavy drum beats may alternate with light ones: BOOM boom, BOOM boom. In a word of many syllables, it would be hard *not* to have a second stress. Here are some examples:

impossibility	im·POSS·i·*BIL*·i·ty
indicator	*IN*·di·CA·tor
Japanese	JAP·an·*ESE*
population	POP·u·*LA*·tion

Usually one of the stresses is a little stronger than the other. *Impossibility*, for example, has somewhat heavier stress on *-bil-* than it does on *-poss-*. *Indicator* has a slightly heavier stress on *in-* than it does on *-ca-*. But it is not important in spelling to be able to tell these degrees of difference between one stress and another, as long as you can tell which syllables are stressed, as opposed to syllables not stressed at all.

You may have to practice awhile listening for stress and identifying the syllables on which it falls before you are sure of it. Just remember that if a word is already familiar to you, you don't have to worry about where the stress *ought* to go. You only have to pronounce the word normally, and listen for where the stress already is.

To make matters even easier, you also don't need to worry about the exact division of syllables. For example, you may not be sure whether the word *normal* is divided as *nor·mal* or as *norm·al*. This variation really makes no difference in identifying the stress. The vowel is the center of the syllable, and not the consonants. It is the vowel which actually is stressed. All you need to do, then, is to identify the vowel of the stressed syllable. This vowel will be the same whether you say "NORmal" or "NORMal."

If you are writing and have to divide a word at the end of a line, or if you want to divide a word into syllables to help you remember the spelling, here are some simple rules to follow:

1. If two consonants come together, divide the word between them:

happen	hap·pen
normal	nor·mal
riddle	rid·dle
succeed	suc·ceed

2. If there is a long open vowel sound, divide between the vowel and the next letter:

cable	ca·ble
locate	lo·cate
propeller	pro·pel·ler

vacation   va·ca·tion (NOT *"vac·a·tion."* This division appears to make a short-vowel syllable, *"vac."*)

3. If there is a short vowel, pronounce the word to see if the following consonant goes with that vowel, making a closed syllable:

punishment   pun·ish·ment (NOT *"pu·ni·shment"*)

continue   con·tin·ue (NOT *"con·ti·nue"*)

4. Divide between root words and suffixes:

spelling   spell·ing (NOT *"spel·ling"*)

5. Never divide a vowel digraph:

unpleasing   un·pleas·ing (NOT *"un·ple·asing"*)

6. Never divide a single-syllable word:

stop   (NOT *"st·op"*)

7. Never carry a single letter over to the next line:

handy   (NOT *"hand·y"*)

These rules may not cover all cases. For example, you may be uncertain about which syllable you should put a consonant with in a long word. When in doubt, consult the dictionary. It will show you where to make the division.

Now find the stressed syllables in each of the following words. The same list is printed three times. The first list shows each word as it ordinarily appears in print. Read each word aloud in a natural voice, as you ordinarily say it. The second list shows the same words divided into syllables. Pronounce them aloud again, and underline the syllable which you naturally stress when speaking. Don't try to exaggerate. Just listen for the stress which is normally there in your pronunciation. If it is difficult for you to listen to yourself, have someone read the words to you. Finally, check your answers with the third list. The stressed syllables are printed in capital letters. Cover the last list with a piece of paper until you are ready to check your answers.

decide	distribute	distribution
temper	harmony	stupidity
display	resident	microscopic
invite	microscope	testimony
slender	reproduce	anniversary
de·cide	dis·trib·ute	dis·tri·bu·tion
tem·per	har·mon·y	stu·pid·i·ty
dis·play	res·i·dent	mi·cro·scop·ic
in·vite	mi·cro·scope	tes·ti·mo·ny
slen·der	re·pro·duce	an·ni·ver·sa·ry
de·CIDE	dis·TRIB·ute	DIS·tri·*BU*·tion
TEM·per	HAR·mon·y	stu·PID·i·ty
dis·PLAY	RES·i·dent	MI·cro·*SCOP*·ic
in·VITE	MI·cro·scope	*TES*·ti·MO·ny
SLEN·der	RE·pro·*DUCE*	AN·ni·*VER*·sa·ry

26· HOW STRESS AFFECTS SPELLING

Heavy stress on one syllable gives that syllable distinctness and clarity. The vowel sound is clear and unmistakable; you can usually spell it by ear. But unstressed syllables are slurred over rapidly. The vowel sound is often spoken so rapidly and becomes so indistinct that you cannot be sure what letter should be used to spell it. Unstressed vowels often become only a kind of grunting sound: "uh." They sound so much alike that they are called "neutral" vowel sounds, no matter whether they are spelled with *a, e, i, o,* or *u.*

The word *normal,* for example, is stressed on the first syllable: "NOR·mal." There is no question of how to spell the syllable *nor-.* It is spelled just as it sounds. But the last syllable, *-mal,* is not stressed at all. Therefore it does not get the same full pronunciation of its vowel sound. Instead, the vowel is hurried over and sounds more like "mul" than "mal."

Many people have been taught to pronounce a word slowly syllable by syllable as an aid in spelling. This method does help to a great extent, for it is easier to take a long word piece by piece and match spelling to pronunciation as you go. But it does not help, unfortunately, in spelling the unstressed vowels.

For example, which of the following spellings is correct?

catagory category catigory

The first syllable, **cat-**, is easy and regular. So are the last two syllables **-gor-** and **-y.** But in the middle is an unstressed vowel with the neutral sound "uh." No matter how slowly and carefully you pronounce the word, you cannot tell from pronunciation alone what letter to use to spell this sound. You have no choice but to rely on sight memory. The correct spelling is:

category

No one would make the mistake of spelling this word *"cutegory"* or *"cotegory,"* because the vowel in that stressed first syllable is very clearly a short *a,* not *u* or *o.* The only spelling problem in this word is its unstressed vowel.

The spelling of many other words becomes much more understandable when you learn to tell the difference between stressed and unstressed syllables. Here is a list of words which, like **category,** are sometimes misspelled simply because of an unstressed vowel:

privilege
separate
similar
stabilize
repetition

The first three of these words, in fact, are among the twenty words most often misspelled by college students. The mistake lies in not remembering which letter to use for an unstressed vowel. Which are the unstressed vowels in the words above? Are there more than one in any of them?

Modern dictionaries now recognize the fact that unstressed vowels are not given the pure pronunciation that stressed vowels have. *a*, *e*, *i*, *o*, and *u*, when not stressed, all sound alike. The dictionaries therefore have adopted a new letter to show the pronunciation of the neutral vowel sound, which is pronounced "uh." This is the letter *e* printed upside down: "ə."

For example, after the dictionary gives the correct spelling of the word *about*, it will also show how it is pronounced:

ə·bout

You are most familiar with the neutral unstressed sound "ə" ("uh") in the word *a* ("a street," "a river") and at the ends of words like *Cuba, Africa, China, Canada, mama, Linda*. In the middle of a word, you will most often find an *i* for the sound "ə":

accident	criminal	hypocrisy	policy
admiral	definite	instigate	politics
alimony	detriment	manifest	primitive
anticipate	difficult	medicine	privilege
animal	easily	military	prodigal
approximate	editor	notify	purity
calamity	eliminate	officer	sacrifice
cannibal	experiment	optimism	sentiment
capital	family	original	similar
contaminate	festival	pertinent	solitude

Somewhat less common is the unstressed *e*:

adequate	different	symmetry
beneficial	element	tapestry
benefit	enemy	tendency
category	interest	tenement
comedy	mathematics	vinegar
currency	repetition	

The most common words with unstressed *a* are:

academic	fundamental	propaganda
adamant	melancholy	relative
comparative	obstacle	senator
emphasize	ornament	separate
explanation	permanent	summary
fallacy	prevalent	testament

The **melan-** in **melancholy** has nothing to do with the melon you eat. It comes from the ancient Greek word for "black."

Unstressed **o** and **u** retain more of their own distinctive pronunciation and are less often confused with the other unstressed vowels:

abdomen	melody	conjugal	occupy
anatomy	memory	impudent	ocular
apology	opposite	luxury	popular
colony	sociology	muscular	regulate
ebony			

27·SOME COMMON SUFFIXES THAT SOUND ALIKE BECAUSE THEY ARE NOT STRESSED

As you have already seen, unstressed syllables may sound exactly alike even though they are spelled with different vowels. *If they were stressed in pronunciation, they would not all sound alike*—they would have a definite long or short vowel sound rather than the neutral sound "ə." It is the lack of stress that makes them lose their individuality and become identical.

A good example is the case of the two suffixes **-able** and **-ible.** These two word-endings have vowels that sound exactly alike. The vowels **a** and **i,** being unstressed, become neutral and lose their identity. The **i** is neither long nor short, as it is when stressed in words like **Bible** or **dribble.** The **a** is neither long nor short, as it is in **table** or **rabble.** Instead, both are pronounced with the nondescript sound "uh," which the dictionaries show by the symbol "ə."

Since these two suffixes cannot be told apart in pronunciation, you are again thrown back on sight memory for correct spelling:

dependable	accessible
detectable	divisible
excitable	possible
memorable	sensible

In Part II of this book you will find lists of words with these suffixes, together with an explanation of why they are spelled that way and with a few practical hints on how some of them can be more easily remembered.

Other pairs of endings that sound alike are *-ent* and *-ant*, *-ence* and *-ance*:

dependent	abundant
evident	ignorant
excellent	important
innocent	tolerant
dependence	abundance
evidence	ignorance
excellence	importance
innocence	tolerance

Lists of words with these endings will also be found in Part II, along with some hints for keeping them straight.

The lack of stress on suffixes also causes certain other common endings to be pronounced with a neutral vowel sound, rather than with the true long or short sound they would have if they were stressed. The word *certain* is an example. If the last syllable were stressed, it would contain a long *a* and would rhyme with *pain*. But instead it has only the neutral sound "ə."

Britain	curtain
captain	fountain
certain	mountain

Contrast these words with ones in which the ending is stressed. The stressed endings receive the long *a* sound, as you would expect from the spelling:

disdain	maintain
entertain	retain

The reason words like *notice* and *practice* do not have a long *i* sound (rhyming with *mice*) is also that the final syllable is not stressed. *Device* and *entice,* on the other hand, do have a long vowel in the last syllable because the stress is placed there.

Other endings which seem to have long vowels, but are not pronounced that way because they are not stressed, are *-ive* and *-ine*.

active	determine
comparative	engine
detective	examine
effective	imagine
olive	medicine

Contrast them with the following words, in which the ending is stressed and therefore has a long-vowel sound:

alive	combine
contrive	divine
deprive	refine

Part II of this book will guide you in the spelling of many other unstressed endings.

28· ERRORS—EXCUSABLE AND INEXCUSABLE

Much that baffles and bewilders people about spelling comes from the fact that unstressed vowels are slurred over in speaking and all sound alike. This slurring leads people to confuse *effect* and *affect*, and to spell *dormitory* with an *a* instead of an *i*. No one needs to worry how to spell *dorm-*, or the last two syllables, *-tory*. It is only the unstressed vowel in the middle which has to be memorized. You don't have to memorize every letter in every word—only those parts of the word which might be confused with something else. It is no disgrace to spell *dormitory* with an *a* by mistake. If you use the word often enough you will soon remember that the right letter is *i*. But it *is* a disgrace to spell it "*dromitory*." There is no reason why the stressed syllable, *dorm-*, should not be spelled exactly as it sounds, rather than "*drom-*"—which is not the way it should sound.

Likewise, it is excusable to misspell **retreat** as *"retreet"* until you learn that **ea** is the right digraph for this word, since both **ea** and **ee** are possible spellings for a long **e.** But if you spelled it *"retret,"* you would be making an inexcusable error. The syllable **-et** can have only a short-vowel sound, not a long one.

An inexcusable error is one which gives a word the wrong pronunciation when it is read aloud the way it is spelled.

29· A PRACTICAL HINT FOR REMEMBERING THE SPELLING OF UNSTRESSED VOWELS

Sometimes two words are derived from the same root word, but the two forms are not stressed on the same syllable:

STAbilize   staBILity

Notice that the syllable **sta-** gets a full long **a** sound in **stabilize.** But **-bil-**, in the same word, gets only a neutral, unclear sound—"bul"—because it is not stressed.

In **stability**, the stress has shifted to **-bil-**. Here, **-bil-** gets a clear, full short **-i** sound because it is stressed; while **sta-** in turn loses its long **a** sound and becomes "stə," because it is not stressed.

When spelling the word **stabilize,** you may forget exactly what letter to use for that unstressed vowel in the middle. But remind yourself of its companion word, **stability,** where the stress shifts to that vowel and shows it up very clearly as an **i.**

Many other words also fall into such pairs:

author	(authər)	authority
definite	(defənite)	define, definitive
emphasize	(emphəsize)	emphatic
grammar	(grammər)	grammatical
hypocrisy	(hypocrəsy)	hypocritical
opposite	(oppəsite)	oppose
politics	(polətics)	political
relative	(relətive)	relate

30· HOW STRESS AFFECTS THE DOUBLING OF CONSONANTS

You know that a final consonant is doubled in order to preserve a short vowel whenever a suffix is added that otherwise would change the vowel to a long one:

begin	beginning
fit	fitting
prefer	preferring
sad	saddest

Notice that in every case the suffix is added to a syllable which is stressed. (A one-syllable word is, of course, a stressed syllable because it has no place else for a stress to fall.)

But if the stress does *not* fall on the last syllable, there is no need to double the consonant:

answer	answered
benefit	benefited
confer	conference
prefer	preference
prison	prisoner
profit	profited
visit	visited

Test yourself by adding the suffix *-ed* to each of the following words. Some will require the final consonant to be doubled, others will not. Do not double the final consonant unless the stress falls on the last syllable.

equip	differ	defer	render
occur	compel	remit	fester

For correct answers, see page 57.

A borderline case: **Transfer** is not pronounced with the same stress by all speakers. Some say "TRANSfer," others "transFER." If we followed the rule for doubling the final **r** according to stress, some would double it, others would not. In such a conflicting state of affairs, the following spellings may be adopted as always correct:

transferred	transferable
transferring	transferal
	transference

31· PREFIXES

Root words can be extended by adding suffixes to the end. They can also be extended in the other direction by adding prefixes to the beginning.

Unlike a suffix, a prefix does not affect the spelling of the root word. The reason is that it comes before the root word. The spelling of any part of a word is always affected by what follows. For example, it is the consonant *following* a vowel which keeps the vowel short—not the consonant that precedes the vowel. Therefore much attention has been paid in this book to the last syllables in words and to the suffixes added onto them. A prefix standing at the beginning of a word will not change the spelling of the root word.

The word **prefix** itself contains the prefix **pre-**, which means "in front of." A prefix is therefore something which is fixed or fastened in front of a word. You are familiar with the prefix **pre-** in many other words also:

prehistoric: before history was written
prepaid: paid in advance
precaution: care, or caution, taken in advance

The words **historic, paid,** and **caution** are unaffected in spelling by the addition of this prefix.

pre- was originally a prefix in the Latin language; but nowadays it is attached freely to many words. We speak of **pre-Civil War, pre-Revolutionary, preelection, predawn.** And in every case, the spelling of the root word is not changed by the addition of this prefix.

If a prefix happens to end with the same consonant that begins the root word, two identical letters will come together:

mis   spell

misspell

over   reach

overreach

un   necessary

unnecessary

The doubling here is not done to preserve the short sound of any vowel. The two letters come together only by accident. Compare the words above with the following ones, whose roots begin with a consonant different from the one in the prefix:

mis   matched

mismatched

over   come

overcome

un   fed

unfed

These prefixes are the same as the ones in the preceding three examples, but this time there is no doubling. Doubling occurs in some words only because two identical letters happen to come together.

Doubling can also occur with vowels. The prefix *co-*, for example, can be added to root words beginning with *o*:

co   operate

cooperate

co   ordinate

coordinate

The double *o* here is not a digraph to be pronounced "oo," as in *hoop* and *groom*. The two separate *o*'s must both be pronounced —one in the prefix, one in the root word.

Another common prefix ending with a vowel is **re-**. When added
to words beginning with **e,** it also forms a doubled vowel:

> re educate
> reeducate
>
> re employ
> reemploy
>
> re enlist
> reenlist

The double **e** here is not a digraph for long **e,** as it is in *green*
and *feel.* Again, the two vowels must be pronounced separately.
One **e** belongs to the prefix and the other **e** to the root word.

Many words, however, came from Latin into English a long
time ago with a prefix already attached. We borrowed the whole
word, prefix and all. We seldom any longer recognize that such
words consist of a root word with a prefix. The word **predict** is a
good example. The root portion, **-dict,** comes from the Latin verb
dicere, which means "to say." Therefore, **predict** means to "say
before"—to say that something is going to happen before it does
happen. This root has also entered into many other English words
with the basic meaning of "speaking" or "saying." For example,
we also have **dictate, dictation, diction,** and **dictionary.** But
"dict" by itself is not a separate English word. It is therefore not
so obvious that **pre-** has been added to a root word.

During the centuries Latin prefixes blended with their root
words until they sometimes became almost unrecognizable to modern spellers. Such prefixes have been frozen into their words and no
longer seem like separate units that can be freely attached to the
beginning of any other root word. In fact, many Latin prefixes
are dead to us; we no longer use them to form new words in
English. Some other prefixes are still alive, because we still use
them to form new words. Two such live prefixes are **re-** and **inter-.**
We can still create words like **reenter, recall, reconstruct;** or
interoffice, intergroup, intercultural. When such live prefixes
are used, we recognize them easily, because we are accustomed to
fastening them freely onto root words. And if they accidentally
create the doubling of consonants, it is easy to see the reason why.

We can identify the root word and its prefix as two separate parts.

However, when the doubling of a consonant occurred many centuries ago by the blending of a prefix with a now unfamiliar root word, we no longer recognize it as an example of the very same kind of doubling.

The word *assimilate* illustrates this fact. It was formed in Latin by adding the prefix *ad-* to the root *similare. ad-* meant "to," and *similare* meant "to make like." But over a long period of time, the *d* of *ad-* was slurred over in speaking until it was blended with the *s* that followed it. In spelling it was eventually replaced by another *s*: *ad-* became *as-*. This change is the reason why we no longer recognize the presence of the prefix *ad-* in this word. Instead of *"adsimilate,"* the word has become *assimilate.*

The *d* of *ad-* also blended with other consonants. *Annex, arrive, attract, abbreviate,* and *appoint,* all originally began with the prefix *ad-*. But in each case, the *d* merged with the consonant that followed it. When the *d* dropped out, the following consonant replaced it.

In not all cases, however, was the *d* changed. In *admire,* for example, the *d* did not blend with the *m.* Whether it blended or didn't blend probably was determined by ease of pronunciation.

The spelling of any part of a word is affected by what follows it—not by what goes before it. A prefix does not influence the spelling of the root word following it. But the root word *does* reach back and influence the spelling of the prefix.

Many other prefixes have, like *ad-,* undergone a change in spelling and have been assimilated into a root word. The result is always a double consonant. For example, the prefix *com-* has changed to *col-* before root words beginning with *l*:

> collapse
> collect
> collide

com- has changed to *cor-* before *r*:

> correct
> correspond
> correlate

Likewise, the prefix *in-* has changed to *il-* and *ir-*:

illegal	irrational
illegible	irregular
illiterate	irresponsible

It would be too difficult for you to remember all the Latin prefixes and the different forms they have taken in modern words. But at least now you know where to expect the doubling of consonants, and why. Doubling occurs most regularly in one of two places: at the end of a prefix and at the beginning of a suffix. The preceding sentence contains three illustrations: *occurs*, *beginning*, and *suffix*. *Occurs* and *suffix* are both examples of the assimilation of a prefix from Latin. *Occurs* has the hidden prefix *ob-*, whose *b* has changed to a *c* before a root word beginning with *c*. *Suffix* has the hidden Latin prefix *sub-*, whose *b* has changed to *f*. *Beginning* has doubled the *n* before the suffix *-ing*, which begins with a vowel.

Below are several examples of often-misspelled words that can be mastered by a knowledge of prefixes:

Professor — The prefix is *pro-*, the same as in *profile* and *project*. The *f* is not doubled, because there is no reason for it to be doubled. The prefix ends in *o*, the root begins with *f*.

Recommend — Two prefixes have been added to a root word, one on top of the other. To the root portion, *-mend* (from the Latin *mandare*, "to entrust"), has been added the prefix *com-*, giving us *commend*. Then another prefix, *re-*, has been added to *commend*, giving us *recommend*. Since the prefix *re-* ends in *e*, there is no reason for the *c* to be doubled.

Accommodate — Here, again, two prefixes have been added to a single root word. Beginning with *mode*, we add *com-* to produce *commode*. Then we add a second prefix, *ad-*, whose *d* has changed to a *c* in the process of time. With the suffix *-ate* attached at the end, we finally have *accommodate*. There is a reason for doubling the *c* and the *m*.

Exaggerate — Even the frequently misspelled word *exaggerate* can be conquered by knowledge of prefixes. It comes from the Latin word **exaggeratus,** "heaped up." The original root is **geratus.** To this root was added our old acquaintance **ad-,** whose **d** was changed to **g** by influence of the **g** that followed it. Then the prefix **ex-** was added to that new word. From **ex** + **ad** + **geratus** we have evolved the word **exaggerate,** with a double **g** that seems illogical until we know how it came about. Usually, **gg** has a hard sound:

bigger   wiggle   ragged

Exaggerate and **suggest** are, in fact, the only two words in the English language which give **gg** the soft pronunciation.

Watch out for common words which are *not* examples of assimilation after a Latin prefix. Below are several groups of words whose first syllables sound alike. Because of this similarity, a consonant is sometimes left out of the words on the left by mistake, while it is incorrectly doubled in the ones on the right.

DOUBLE THESE:		LEAVE THESE SINGLE:	
acclaim	ac·claim	across	a·cross
appear	ap·pear	agree	a·gree
approach	ap·proach	amount	a·mount
arrange	ar·range	arise	a·rise
attract	at·tract	around	a·round
opponent	op·po·nent	arouse	a·rouse
opportunity	op·por·tun·i·ty	operate	op·er·ate
oppose	op·pose	opinion	o·pin·ion
immediate	im·me·di·ate	image	im·age
immense	im·mense	imagination	im·ag·i·na·tion

Not one commonly used word in your dictionary begins **omm-.** If a first syllable begins with **om-,** you can be sure it has only one **m**:

omit   o·mit

32· UNSTRESSED VOWELS IN PREFIXES

You have seen the problem of spelling an unstressed vowel in suffixes such as **-able** and **-ible,** and in the middle of a word such as **category.** The problem occurs less often at the beginning of words, for the simple reason that the beginning is more often stressed.

Only a few words cause any real difficulty. These words begin with **en-** or **in-,** **de-** or **di-.** Short *e* and short *i* are hard to tell apart in pronunciation even when they are stressed. Chances are that in rapid speaking you say *pin* and *pen* almost identically. Many words begin with the prefixes **in-** or **en-:**

inability	infinite	enable	enjoy
inaccurate	inflate	enact	enlarge
inactive	inform	enchant	enlist
inadequate	inhale	enclose	enrage
incapable	inspire	encourage	enrich
incline	install	encroach	entrust
include	intend	endear	
incorrect	interest	endorse	
increase	invent	endure	
inedible	invest	enforce	
inept	invisible	engage	
infect	involve	engrave	

Several points may help you keep **in-** and **en-** straight:

> **in-** is far more common than **en-**;
>
> **en-** is mainly a prefix used to form verbs of action, in which the root word is quite clear: **en·rich, en·able, en·trust;**
>
> **in-** often cannot be detached from a verb to leave a recognizable root word: **inhale, inspire, include** (contrast with **en·rich, en·trust**);
>
> **in-** often means "not," while **en-** never does: **inactive, invisible, inaccurate.**

Only four common words can be spelled with either **in-** or **en-:**

enclose	endorse	ensure	entrust
inclose	indorse	insure	intrust

Insure has now become the common word used in business, while **ensure** has come to mean simply "to make certain."

Because *in-* sometimes means "not," it is also likely to be confused with *un-*. But *un-* is a very live prefix and far more commonly used as a negative than is *in-*. No more than a few dozen words in common usage use *in-* as a negative prefix, whereas those beginning with *un-* run into the thousands.

Here are two helpful distinctions:

unequal	*but*	inequality
unable	*but*	inability

Learn the few words in the above lists that *must* begin with *in-*, and use *un-* for everything else.

The prefix *dis-* implies the reversal of the meaning of the root word:

disabled	disconnect	dislike
disadvantage	discontinue	disloyal
disagree	discount	disobey
disappear	discourage	disorderly
disapprove	disfavor	displace
disbelieve	dishearten	displease
discolor	dishonest	disrespectful
discomfort	disintegrate	distasteful

dis- appears as the prefix to many a Latin root word, even though that root may no longer be recognizable as a separate word:

disaster	disdain	dispel	disrupt
discern	disease	dispense	distant
discriminate	disgrace	disperse	distort
discussion	disgust	display	distribute

The *s* is never doubled unless it happens to come together with a root word also beginning with an *s*:

dissatisfied	dissociate	dissonance
dissimilar	dissolve	dissuade

The prefix **dis-** is sometimes confused with words that happen to begin with **des-:**

describe   desire   despise
design   despair   destroy

These six words are the only ones in common usage and can be easily memorized.

A few words beginning with **di-** are sometimes misspelled **de-** because of the unstressed vowel:

divine   divide   divorce

Ridiculous begins with **ri-**, not **re-**. Associate it with the stressed syllable in **ridicule**.

33· COMPOUND WORDS

We have seen how easy it is to build words in English by adding prefixes and suffixes. In addition to this method of forming words, we have another: that of compounding, or combining two root words into one. Words like **postman, houseboat,** and **beefsteak** are made not by adding prefixes or suffixes, but by combining two root words:

post + man
house + boat
beef + steak

Compound words are simple to spell, because both the root words retain their own original spellings without change. If the consonant at the end of the first one is the same as the consonant at the beginning of the second, then two identical letters will fall together. No letters are dropped or changed:

newsstand   (NOT "new·stand")
roommate   (NOT "roo·mate")

Compound words can be easily identified by the fact that when they are taken apart, their parts can stand alone as separate words.

Divide the following compounds into the original words from which they have been made:

watermelon   blowtorch
birthday   toehold
trademark   hedgehog

34· SUMMARY OF REGULAR SPELLING

Spelling begins with the two kinds of sounds: vowels and consonants. Your basic vocabulary consists of thousands of simple one-syllable words that have either a long or a short vowel. After learning how to spell those vowel sounds, you can build words and syllables into longer words by adding prefixes and suffixes, all according to regular principles that determine whether consonants will be doubled or not.

Much of the seeming irregularity of spelling disappears when we see the way words are put together. All the minor exceptions to the rules are far less important than these basic principles of word-formation. Study Part I of this book over and over until you are sure that you can spell all the words in the tests and examples without mistakes. You will find yourself free from painfully having to memorize every single word letter by letter as if it were totally different from every other word. You will be able to spell and pronounce countless words you have never seen before because they will fit familiar patterns. Your vocabulary will be more precise because you will be able to see how one word is related to another through their common root. You may even find that you can read with greater speed and accuracy.

The remainder of this book covers first the minor variations in spelling and then the relatively few words that are downright irregularities. Understanding these variations and irregularities depends on how well you have learned the basic principles in Part I.

ANSWERS TO TESTS IN PART I

Page 4: Short and long vowel sounds

SHORT:	LONG:
skim	brave
fret	hive
box	rose
ham	fuse
bug	scene

Page 14: Digraphs: ha*ng*ing   wa*sh*ing
                    bo*th*er   ri*ch*est

Separate sounds:

hot·house   gos·hawk   van·guard   ant·hill

Page 16: Adding suffixes

| debating | spitting | telling | exciting |
| blasting | shining | roving | winning |

| debatable | detestable |
| likable | usable |

saddest	rarest
whitest	blandest
thinnest	

Page 46: Adding suffixes

| equipped | differed | deferred | rendered |
| occurred | compelled | remitted | festered |

PART II

Word-Endings

The beginning parts of words are easier to spell than their endings. For one thing, most words are stressed at the beginning and seldom at the end. Probably no more than one-tenth of the words on any printed page are stressed on the last syllable. As you know, unstressed syllables are unclear in pronunciation and harder to spell by ear. Many words therefore have endings that sound alike even though they are spelled differently.

Second, suffixes are more numerous than prefixes. We use word-endings much more often to extend or change a meaning than we do prefixes. Prefixes tend to take their place quietly without disturbing the word, but suffixes often upset the root word by requiring the doubling, adding, or dropping of letters to preserve the right pronunciation.

Third, not all final syllables are suffixes. If they are not—for example, in a word like **melon**—the preceding consonant may not be doubled.

Word-endings need your close attention for these reasons:

> Unstressed endings may sound alike but be spelled differently.
> Consonants must be doubled in simple words when suffixes are added.
> All final syllables are not necessarily suffixes.

In Part II word-endings are arranged by groups with these three reasons in mind. You will not have to face a mass of exceptions and irregularities: everything you have learned still applies. You will be learning how to extend your knowledge to cover most of the words you will ever read or need to write. The true exceptions and irregularities are taken up in Parts III and IV.

35· DOUBLE CONSONANTS AT THE END OF A WORD: -ff, -ss, -ll

A regular short-vowel syllable ordinarily does not end in a doubled consonant:

WRONG: matt   gett   fitt   rott   cutt

Normally it ends in a single consonant:

RIGHT: mat   get   fit   rot   cut

Three letters, however,—*f*, *s*, and *l*—are an exception to this regularity. They are normally doubled at the end of words following a short vowel.

-ff ||||||||||||||||||||||||||||||||||||||||||||||||||||||||

staff	cliff	off	buff	bailiff
stiff	doff	cuff	plaintiff
skiff	scoff	guff	tariff
tiff		muff	sheriff
whiff		puff	

Most of these are one-syllable words. But even the two-syllable words in the right-hand column have an *-ff* following a short vowel. At the end of a word, *f* is doubled following a short vowel.

REMEMBER: *f* is not doubled after *every* short vowel—only when it comes at the end of a word. For example, below are three words in which a single *f* follows a short vowel—but not at the end of the word:

*af*ter   re*f*erence   speci*f*ic

Everywhere else, then, *f* behaves like other consonants. It is never doubled after a long vowel:

waif   reef   leaf   goof

It may be doubled earlier in the word when it is part of a prefix, as explained in Section 31:

The Latin prefix **sub-** turns into **suf-** when the root word begins with an **f**:

suffix   sufficient   suffer   suffuse

Likewise, the Latin prefix **ad-** may turn into **af-**:

affix   afflict   affirm   afford

And the prefix **ex-** may turn into **ef-**:

efface   effect   efficient   effort

The only place where **f** is not as regular as any other consonant is at the end of a word following a short vowel. There it is always doubled.

At this point, someone is sure to notice that the word **if** is an exception to this regular principle. But then no one is likely to misspell this common word. A few other exceptions are some French words, such as **chef** and **aperitif,** which are spelled according to French rather than English spelling practices.

ss ||||||||||||||||||||||||||||||||||||||||||||||||||||||||||||||||

The letter **s** is also normally doubled at the end of one-syllable, short-vowel words:

brass	dress	bliss	boss	fuss
class	less	kiss	loss	muss
mass	mess	miss	toss	truss

You will find occasional EXCEPTIONS. For example:

gas	plus	us
bus	pus	yes
		this

Gas and **bus,** however, are shortened forms of **gasoline** and **omnibus** and do not double their **s** because it is not doubled in the original word. **Pus** and **plus** are taken directly from Latin with no change in spelling. **Us, yes,** and **this,** like **if,** are the few real exceptions, but are so frequently used that they cause no problem.

The letter *s* is also normally doubled (just as *f* was) at the ends of longer words when the final syllable has a short vowel:

address	dismiss
carcass	embarrass
caress	emboss
cutlass	harass
discuss	surpass

But, again, we have a group of exceptions from foreign languages. These exceptions are words which were borrowed from Latin or Greek. They did not end in *-ss* in those languages, so they do not have a double *s* in English now:

analysis	bonus
basis	calculus
crisis	census
emphasis	circus

Like the letter *f*, *s* is also doubled in the usual expected places. It is found doubled at the end of a prefix in words of Latin origin, in which *ad-* has been assimilated and changed to *as-*.

assault	assert	associate
assemble	assess	assume
assent	assign	assure

The double *s* is retained in compound words whose root word ends in *-ss*:

dressmaker	classroom	passport

A useful tip: The prefix **mis-** has only one *s*. It is not the word *"miss"* attached to the beginning of other words. It is a separate prefix with a meaning of its own, "wrong" or "bad":

misfit	mislead
misinform	mispronunciation
mislabel	misspell

II |||||||||||||||||||||||||||||||||||||||||||||||||||||||||||

Like *f* and *s, l* is also normally doubled at the end of one-syllable, short-vowel words:

all	bell	ill	doll	bull
ball	fell	fill	loll	full
call	sell	kill	moll	gull
tall	tell	will		pull

But *l* is different from *f* and *s* in this one respect: it is NOT doubled at the end of words of *more* than one syllable:

total	travel	until	idol	careful
legal	camel	devil	pistol	wonderful
animal	cancel	pupil	carol	useful
local	level	civil		teaspoonful
formal	mackerel	pencil		
opal	parallel			

If you are among the many people confused by the word **parallel,** you now have an easy way to remember it. The final *l* must be single, since words of more than one syllable do not double the final *l.*

The suffix *-ful* (meaning "full" or "filled with") is always spelled with a single *l.* Don't confuse it with the separate word *full,* which ends in *-ll* like other one-syllable, short-vowel words such as *hull* or *pull.*

Notice also that *until* is spelled with only a single *l,* while the alternative form *till* is spelled with a double *l. Till* is a one-syllable, short-vowel word like *hill* or *pill* and therefore doubles the *l.*

When a prefix is added to one of these single-syllable root words ending in *-ll,* the double *l* is retained:

call	fill	sell
recall	refill	oversell

These new words have two syllables, to be sure; but they are different from the two-syllable words above that end in *-l.* Those words (like **travel** and **total**) were *not* formed from a one-syllable root word that had a double *l* to begin with. If you think **until** is an exception, look it up in your dictionary. You will find that **until** was not made by simply adding **un-** to **till.** Both **till** and **until** are very old words which have long been separate.

Likewise, the double *l* remains when suffixes are added:

illness   willful   tallest

and when compound words are created:

ballpoint   bulldog

A COMMON ERROR: Correct usage does not recognize the word *"alright."* It is two separate words, **all right.**

A Few Oddities ||||||||||||||||||||||||||||||||||||||||||||||||||||||||||||||||

A few scattered common words end in doubled letters other than *f, s,* or *l*:

ebb	add	egg	burr	buzz
	odd		err	

A useful tip: Don't confuse **add** with **ad,** the shortened form of **advertisement.**

36· WORDS ENDING IN -ck

QUICK REVIEW: *c* and *k* both have the same sound. *c,* however, has the "s" sound before *e* and *i,* as in **cell** and **city;** but everywhere else it has a "k" sound.

One-syllable words in which a "k" sound follows a short vowel are always spelled with **-ck,** rather than with **-c** or **-k** alone:

back	beck	lick	dock	buck
crack	deck	pick	lock	duck
lack	neck	tick	mock	luck
track	peck	wick	pock	struck

We never spell these words with only a *-c* or a *-k*:

WRONG:

bac   nec

bak   nek

We never spell them with *-cc* or *-kk*:

WRONG:

bacc   necc

bakk   nekk

Instead, we combine *c* and *k* to perform the job of a double consonant:

back   neck

After all, *c* and *k* at the end of a word both have the same sound. Together, they operate like any other doubled consonant. In consonant clusters, *k* alone is usually used to spell this sound. There is no doubling:

milk   thank   stork   dusk

A very few words, like *arc* and *talc,* may spell this sound with a *c.* And, of course, if *k* follows a vowel digraph it is not doubled:

brook   look   took

Words of more than one syllable do not double the final *c*:

almanac	frolic	plastic
attic	havoc	relic
critic	phonic	tonic
frantic	picnic	toxic

Most of the words above have the same ending: *-ic,* a suffix which means "characterized by" or "having the nature of" something. For example, *allergic* means having the character or nature of an allergy. Some other words with this suffix are:

alcoholic	nostalgic
astronomic	specific
electronic	terrific

This suffix accounts for most of the words of more than one syllable which end in **-c.**

EXCEPTIONS: As is always the case, a few words refuse to be consistent (but not without a reason). *Sac* and *tic* are technical words borrowed from French. *Sac,* meaning in French a "little bag," is used in biology to denote a small pouch in a plant or animal that contains fluid. And *tic* is a medical term meaning a spasmodic twitching of a muscle. The word *attack* is an exception to the group of two-syllable words which ordinarily end in **-c** rather than **-ck.** A few other exceptions are two-syllable words ending in **-ock**:

bullock	hemlock
buttock	hillock
cassock	hummock
haddock	mattock
hammock	wedlock

As usual, one-syllable root words may be lengthened by adding a prefix, or by compounding:

unlock	halfback
toothpick	sidetrack

In such cases, the root word—as always—keeps its original spelling.

The same thing is true when suffixes are added:

backing	lucky
cracker	pecked

The root words are all one-syllable, short-vowel words ending in **-ck: *back, crack, peck, luck.***

37· WORDS ENDING IN -ch AND -tch

QUICK REVIEW: A few consonant sounds used in speaking have no letter in our alphabet. In order to spell them, we combine two existing letters. We then treat this digraph, or combination of two letters, as if it stood for one single sound. One such digraph is **ch.** It appears in words like **choose, cheer, lunch,** and **inch.**

The words **lunch** and **inch** are both one-syllable, short-vowel words, with the consonant **n** forming a cluster with the **ch.** The following words are all similar to **lunch** and **inch.** The short vowel is followed by a consonant and a final **ch:**

branch	bench	filch	conch	bunch
march	squelch	finch	scorch	crunch
ranch	stench	lynch	torch	gulch
starch	wench	pinch		lurch

None of the above words with short vowels end in **-tch.** All of them end in **-ch.**

Now look at the short-vowel words below. They all end in **-tch,** rather than **-ch.** In these words there is *no other consonant after the vowel:*

catch	fetch	itch	botch	crutch
latch	wretch	ditch	scotch	Dutch
patch		hitch	notch	hutch

-tch is used instead of **-ch** when no other consonant follows the short vowel.

EXCEPTIONS: A few common words refuse to obey this principle, and are spelled with **-ch** where you would expect **-tch: rich, which, such, much.**

Words of more than one syllable end in **-ch** rather than **-tch:**

attach	ostrich	sandwich

Since **-tch** is used at the end of short-vowel words, you would not expect it to follow long vowels, and it doesn't:

beach	broach
peach	coach
reach	poach
teach	

Following a long vowel, *-ch* is used—never *-tch.*
What to remember:

>Use *-tch* only where the "ch" sound follows a short vowel,
with no other consonant in between. Example: *stitch.*
Use *-ch* after another consonant following a short vowel.
Example: *pinch.*
Use *-ch* after a long vowel:

>>leech   roach

>Use *-ch* at the end of a word of two syllables:

>>detach

A useful tip: Don't confuse *witch* and *which.* You may pronounce *which* exactly like *witch,* leaving out the *h.* Many people
do. But even though the two words may sound alike to you, they
are spelled differently. *Witch* is regular, for it follows the expected pattern of a short-vowel word. *Which* is not so regular:
not only is the *h* silent in many people's pronunciation, but it is
spelled with *-ch* where you would expect *-tch.*

38· WORDS ENDING IN -ge AND -dge

Exactly like words ending in *-ch* and *-tch* are those ending in
-ge and *-dge.*

Where another consonant comes before the *g,* the ending is
-ge:

barge	merge	bilge	forge	bulge
large	serge	singe	gorge	lunge

But when the vowel is short and no other consonant comes before
-ge, d is added (just as *t* was inserted before *-ch*):

badge	edge	bridge	dodge	budge
	hedge	midge	lodge	fudge
	wedge			nudge

When the vowel is long, the ending is simply *-ge*—never *-dge*:

cage   huge
page   stooge
rage
sage
stage

In words of more than one syllable, the ending is also *-ge* (not *-dge*):

college   refuge   percentage
privilege   yardage   postage

THE ONLY EXCEPTIONS: knowledge, acknowledge

In compound words created from a root word that ends in *-dge,* the spelling of the root word is kept:

hedgerow   bridgework

If suffixes or prefixes are added, the *dg* of the root word is also preserved:

dislodge   dodger   wedging

NOTE: The words *judgment* and *acknowledgment* usually omit the *e* after *dg.* However, the more regular spellings *judgement* and *acknowledgement* are recognized as correct also.

Tragedy has no *dg.* There would have to be a root word *"tradge"*—which doesn't exist.

The ending *-age* is another fairly common suffix. It appears on three of the words above. A few more examples of it are:

breakage   orphanage
dosage   tankage

If you are worried about confusing words that end in *-ege* with those that end in *-age,* remember that *-ege* is *not* a suffix. You cannot remove *-ege* from *college* and *privilege* and have a root word left. But you can remove **-age** from the words below and have a familiar root word remaining:

break · age	percent · age
orphan · age	post · age

39· -ce AND -se

Since *c* before *e* has the sound "s," the endings **-ce** and **-se** sound alike and are sometimes confused. But, as usual, only a few words really offer a problem. The rest can be sorted into groups that are not difficult to remember.

First, there is a group of one-syllable words with a long vowel:

a	e	i	o	u
ace	fleece	ice		truce
face	peace	mice		
place	niece	nice		
race	piece	rice		
space		spice		
trace		twice		
base	cease		dose	goose
case	crease			loose
chase	grease			moose
vase	lease			noose

These are all commonly used words, seen so often in print that you probably memorized them long ago. Still, it is interesting to see how the spellings sort themselves out. Only in words with a long *a* sound or a digraph for long *e* is there any significant overlap between **-ce** and **-se** spellings.

The words *rise, wise, rose,* and *ruse* do not count, because they are pronounced with a "z" sound rather than with the hissed "s." The voiced "s" or "z" sound is never spelled with a *c*.

Next, there is a group of short-vowel words of one syllable, in which a consonant comes before the **-ce** or **-se** ending:

a	e	i	o	u
chance	fence	mince	sconce	dunce
dance	hence	prince		
France		since		
trance		wince		
farce				
false	dense	rinse	horse	curse
lapse	sense			purse
sparse	tense			
	hearse			
	verse			
	terse			
	else			

Here, too, the spellings do not overlap very much. Nearly all the *-ce* words end in *-nce,* whereas only four of the *-se* words do. The *-se* words usually have another consonant—*l, p,* or *r*—just before the ending.

Out of all these words, only one pair seems to cause any difficulty:

since   sense

This difficulty occurs only because the two words sound very much alike. The word **sense** can be associated with **sensible** and **sensation** as an easy way to remember its spelling.

Words of more than one syllable are usually considered more difficult, but they are more easily remembered when arranged in groups. First, you can eliminate the dozens of common words ending in *-ance* and *-ence,* which will be given in Section 50— words like **entrance** and **evidence.** Very few words end in *-anse* or *-ense.* Below are the ones you are most likely to come across:

dispense	expense	incense	suspense
expanse	immense	intense	

As a general rule, most words with an *n* before the ending use *-ce:*

convince   evince   pronounce

If a consonant other than **n** comes before the ending, the spelling is normally **-se** rather than **-ce**:

collapse	eclipse
convulse	immerse
disperse	impulse
diverse	rehearse

This grouping leaves the words which have a long-vowel syllable at the end:

erase	decrease	advice	deduce
	increase	device	induce
	release		produce
		concise	reduce
		paradise	
		precise	excuse
			obtuse

The normal ending is **-se.** **Advice** and **device** are the only trouble-makers. Trouble occurs because each has a related verb: **advise** and **devise.** But these verbs are pronounced with a voiced "s," or a "z" sound. They must be spelled with an **s,** for **-ce** never is voiced. Try to remember them as two pairs, in which the hissed "s" is spelled **-ce** and the voiced "s" is spelled **-se**:

advice	advise
device	devise

A few words end with a long-vowel spelling, but are not stressed on that last syllable. Therefore the long-vowel sound is lost and becomes the familiar neutral "uh" sound. These words are spelled with **-ce**:

furnace	notice	lettuce
menace	practice	
necklace	precipice	
palace	prejudice	
preface		
surface		

TWO EXCEPTIONS: purpose, promise

Last, we have four common words which worry many good spellers as well as poor ones, but which are really the easiest of all. They may be spelled with either *-ce* or *-se.* Both are considered correct:

defence	defense
licence	license
offence	offense
pretence	pretense

40· ENDINGS WE DON'T THINK OF AS SUFFIXES: -en and -et

Many words follow our regular pattern of a short-vowel root with an ending which we may not recognize as a suffix:

fasten	chicken	bucket	picket
listen	heathen	cricket	racket
sharpen	kitchen	gadget	thicket
	maiden	jacket	

In each case, the root of the word follows the same principle governing all one-syllable, short-vowel words. The final consonant of the root is doubled before a suffix beginning with a vowel. If a consonant cluster follows the vowel, the vowel is short in such words also. A vowel digraph—as in **maiden** and **heathen**—is long and therefore causes no doubling.

Perhaps you noticed one peculiarity of the combination **st** in these words. Read the following list aloud:

bustle	jostle
fasten	listen
glisten	whistle

The *t* has become silent, leaving only an *s* in pronunciation. We cannot leave the *t* out, however, or the vowel would become long. We need two consonants to keep the vowel short. Logically, we should have *ss* instead of *st.* But the *t* got in there a long time ago for a reason, and has stayed in even though it is now silent.

Some people pronounce the *t* in **often** and **soften** simply because it is there in the spelling; but it is normally silent.

41· WORDS ENDING IN -le

The interesting thing about the common ending *-le* is that it is pronounced backwards. It should be spelled *-el,* for in pronunciation the *l* actually comes at the end with the vowel sound in front of it: "əl."

We have a large group of words with this common ending, and all of them follow the familiar pattern. If the vowel in the root is short, then the consonant is doubled:

battle	heckle	middle	boggle	buckle
hackle	meddle	ripple	bottle	rubble
haggle	settle	sniffle	coddle	scuffle
saddle		wiggle	hobble	struggle

EXCEPTIONS: triple, treble

If the vowel in the root word is long, then the consonant before *-le* is single:

able	bridle	ogle	bugle
maple	idle		
table	rifle		
	title		

These roots therefore behave just like all one-syllable words when a suffix beginning with a vowel is added. If the root has a short vowel, its consonant is doubled before *-le.* If the vowel is long, the consonant remains single. And, logically, if a consonant cluster follows the vowel, the vowel will be short just as it is when a doubled consonant follows it:

dwindle	gargle	spindle
fondle	handle	trample

42· WORDS ENDING IN -re

Only a few words in American spelling end in *-re* rather than
-er:

acre   ogre   mediocre   massacre

These spellings are illogical, like the *-le* ending, for in pronunciation the vowel comes before the *r* rather than after: "ər." Notice
that in each case a *c* or *g* precedes the ending. If these words were
spelled *"acer"* or *"oger,"* the *c* and *g* would have a soft sound.
The reversal of the *r* and *e* keeps *c* and *g* hard.

43· DOUBLE AND SINGLE CONSONANTS IN TWO-SYLLABLE WORDS

Up to this point you have stayed close to the familiar pattern of
one-syllable words that double their consonant after a short vowel
when a suffix is added:

plan	planned
sit	sitting
pig	piggish

You have also become acquainted with many words that double
the consonant before the endings *-le, -en,* and *-et,* even though
the root is not always a separate word:

saddle	barren	mallet
wiggle	chicken	sonnet

You expect a *single* consonant to follow a long vowel:

table	raven
open	rifle

This regular pattern also extends to many other words which do
not have separate roots with a detachable suffix:

LONG VOWELS FOLLOWED BY A SINGLE CONSONANT

agent	decent	bison	bonus	duty
baby	even	climax	focus	future
basin	evil	crisis	grocer	humor
halo	fever	idol	moment	lucid
lady	meter	item	motor	pupil
major	Peter	minor	over	stupid
naked	recent	silent	pony	super
paper	veto	spider	sober	tutor
razor				
wager				

SHORT VOWELS FOLLOWED BY A DOUBLED CONSONANT

ballot	bellow	bitter	bobbin	butter
banner	berry	cribbage	bottom	button
barrel	cherry	dinner	comma	buzzard
cabbage	Emma	gizzard	comment	cunning
clatter	lesson	glimmer	common	funnel
dapper	letter	glitter	dodder	gulley
fallow	mellow	jitter	fodder	mutter
flatter	merry	litter	follow	pulley
happen	message	million	folly	rummage
manner	pennant	minnow	fossil	stubborn
matter	reckon	mitten	hollow	suffer
passive	tennis	pillow	holly	sully
platter	terror	ribbon	jolly	summer
rabbit	vessel	silly	motto	supper
shatter	yellow	twitter	pollen	tunnel
tallow		willow	posse	

There is only one GROUP OF EXCEPTIONS to this regularity—two-syllable words which are spelled with only a single consonant following a short vowel. Examples:

banish	blemish	finish	polish	punish
famish	relish	liver	bodice	study
radish	devil	quiver	novice	bunion
Spanish	level	river	promise	pumice

vanish	rebel	shiver	robin
camel	clever	frigid	model
gravel	ever	rigid	novel
panel	never	timid	solid
travel	sever	vivid	profit
acid	leper	limit	vomit
valid	record	rivet	comet
salad	tenor	linen	proper
cabin	felon	vigor	modern
satin	lemon	city	modest
patent	melon	pity	honest
talent	seven	lily	product
planet	legend	lizard	copy
tavern	second	wizard	body
manage	tenant	sinew	olive
balance	present	widow	homage
statue	venom	ribald	scholar
stature	denim	spinach	potash
shadow	credit	mimic	tonic
atom	tepid	lyric	logic
magic	menace	bigot	closet
panic	preface	spigot	

Two-syllable words, then, that have NOT been formed by adding a suffix to a one-syllable root do not necessarily double the consonant after a short vowel. Some of them do—for example, *manner*, *silly*, and *comment*. But some do not—for example, *camel*, *lily*, and *proper*.

Because a single consonant may follow *either* a short *or* a long vowel in such two-syllable words—though it regularly follows a long one—we have some spellings which may be pronounced with a long vowel in one word but a short vowel in another:

LONG	SHORT	LONG	SHORT
evil	*devil*	*even*	*seven*
nature	*stature*	*navel*	*gravel*
demon	*lemon*	*latent*	*patent*
fever	*never*	*donor*	*honor*

LONG	SHORT	LONG	SHORT
d*iver*	l*iver*	cl*over*	c*over*
		union	b*union*

Two-syllable words are divided into syllables as follows:

SHORT VOWELS (close the short vowel with a consonant)

but·ter	rad·ish
cab·bage	sev·en
mod·ern	ter·ror

LONG VOWELS (leave the long vowel open)

mo·tor	si·lent
pa·per	stu·pid

44· -ed AND -id

-ed is a familiar verb ending for the past tense: ***started, planted, spotted, potted, lifted, patted, rotted.*** The final consonant of the root word is doubled:

rot	rotted
pot	potted

-ed also appears as an ending of a few adjectives:

crooked	naked	sacred
hundred	ragged	wretched
jagged	rugged	wicked

Fortunately, these adjectives all double the consonant after a short vowel just as the verbs do when -*ed* is added:

jagged	ragged	rugged	wicked

Notice that ***crooked*** has only a single **k** because **oo** is a vowel digraph.

Words ending in *-id,* on the other hand, do not double the consonant after a short vowel. *-id* is not a detachable suffix that has been added to a root word. Therefore, the consonant does not have to be doubled. The following words are further examples of two-syllable words which happen to have a single consonant after a short vowel (some examples of such words were given in Section 43):

acid	frigid	rabid	valid
arid	livid	rapid	vapid
florid	placid	rigid	vivid

When the vowel is long, or when there is a consonant cluster, there is no spelling problem. Pronunciation is a safe guide:

fluid	candid
humid	morbid
lucid	sordid
	splendid
	turbid

Many of these adjectives ending in **-id** form a noun by adding the suffix **-ity.** The **d** is never doubled, even though the last syllable before the suffix is stressed:

acidity	rapidity
humidity	rigidity
morbidity	validity

45· -al AND -el; -il AND -ile

The unstressed endings **-al, -el, -il,** and **-ile** are all pronounced alike. They are pronounced "əl," just like the ending **-le** discussed in Section 41.

-al and -el ||||||||||||||||||||||||||||||||||||||||||||||||||||||||||||||||||||||||||||

The ending **-al** is a common suffix. Added to a root, it forms a new word:

betray	betrayal	refuse	refusal
form	formal	spine	spinal
function	functional	tide	tidal

In contrast, the ending **-el** is NOT a suffix added to a root. The following words are further examples of those you were given in

Section 43—two-syllable words which happen to have a single consonant after a short vowel:

rebel	shovel	travel
revel	towel	vowel

The word **nickel,** on the other hand, doubles its consonant according to the regular pattern, even though **-el** is not a suffix. Remember that two-syllable words NOT formed from a root word sometimes have a doubled consonant and sometimes do not. A few others ending in **-el** also double the consonant just as **nickel** does: **tunnel, fennel, pommel, chattel.**

When you are in doubt about whether to spell an ending **-el** or **-al,** leave off the ending and see if you have a familiar root word. If you do, then use **-al.**

While this method will help in many cases, the root word is not always as obvious as it is in each of the words above. For example, the Latin root **mort** (death) gives us **mortal** when the suffix **-al** is added. The root **medic** gives us **medical,** as well as **medicine** and **medication.** The Latin word **totus** (whole or entire) gives us **total**; and **finis** (end) gives us **final.** In these cases, the root word is not a separate familiar English word. When you come across such a word and are unsure of its proper ending, look it up in your dictionary. There you will find not only the correct spelling, but a short explanation of the origin of the word. You will be shown the original Latin root word to which **-al** has been added.

It is far easier to remember the spelling of a word if you know its root and its prefixes or suffixes than if you know only the letters of the alphabet of which it is composed. Knowing the root helps you associate it with other words derived from that same root. It also helps you understand any doubling of consonants that has resulted from adding a prefix or a suffix.

-il and -ile ||||||||||||||||||||||||||||||||||||||||||||||||||||||||||||

A few words end in unstressed **-il** or **-ile,** which sound like the unstressed endings **-le, -el,** and **-al:**

anvil	fossil	docile	hostile
civil	pencil	fertile	missile
daffodil	peril	fragile	textile
devil	tonsil	futile	virile
evil	utensil		

IMPORTANT: Notice again that there is no regular doubling of consonants.

What to remember:

> Words ending in the unstressed sound "əl" are most often one of two kinds:
> (1) Those ending in *-le,* like *battle, riddle, wobble*
> (2) Those ending in the suffix *-al,* like *global, refusal, tidal*

Words ending in *-el, -il,* and *-ile* are in the minority. Always take your chances on the most common spelling first. Recognize the suffixes *-le* and *-al* so that you will know when to double the consonant before the suffix of a short-vowel root word.

Now you are ready for another test. The following words are all taken from the preceding sections in Part II. This time, try testing yourself before you study the words individually. Have someone read the words aloud as you write them. If you miss any, compare your mistakes with the correct spellings and go back to the explanatory sections again to refresh your memory. Then test yourself again, and repeat until you can spell all the words correctly. You can also use the word lists in each section as tests.

chef	misspell	almanac	triple
sheriff	teaspoonful	hostile	haggle
all right	parallel	tonsil	bustle
carcass	barrel	peril	fragile
crisis	communal	nickel	missile
analysis	calculus	until	hammock
witch	roach	judgment	percentage
which	detach	college	since
dispense	precipice	paradise	sense
advice	advise	license (or -ce)	sparse

46· -in AND ›ine; -on AND -an

-in and **-ine** ||||||||||||||||||||||||||||||||||||||||||||||||||||||||||||||

As you have seen in so many instances already, words of two or more syllables are very seldom stressed on the last syllable, causing a loss of the well-defined vowel sound. Thus, endings such as *-il* and *-ile* are pronounced exactly alike. The same is true of words ending with *-in* and *-ine.* If these syllables were stressed, there would be no problem in spelling them. For example:

win	wine
fin	refine
bin	combine

But when they are not stressed, they both sound alike. For example:

robin	engine

Although there is no easy rule for remembering which to use, here are a few pointers that may help:

Most of the words ending with *-in* have two syllables only, and are nouns:

basin	Latin	raisin
bobbin	muslin	robin
cabin	pippin	satin
cousin	poplin	

Notice that most of them do *not* double the consonant after the short vowel, for again we do not have a suffix added to a familiar root word.

Only a few three-syllable nouns end with *-in*:

aspirin	mandolin
javelin	origin

Words ending with *-ine* are mostly three-syllable words. While some are nouns, many are verbs or adjectives:

heroine	discipline	feminine
medicine	examine	genuine
determine	imagine	masculine

Only a few are two-syllable words:

doctrine	engine	famine

-on |||||||||||||||||||||||||||||||||||||||||||||||||||||||||

Another relatively small group of words (mostly nouns) ends in *-on.* Some double the consonant after a short vowel:

cannon	lesson
common	ribbon
cotton	

And some do not:

dragon	lemon	pigeon	talon
felon	melon	prison	weapon

Weapon has a very irregular spelling for the short *e* sound. And *pigeon* has a silent *e* for the purpose of preserving the soft *g* sound.

A few have long vowels:

bacon	python	season	treason
patron	reason	siphon	

Other words with an unstressed *-on* ending are:

abandon	pardon
cinnamon	salmon
criterion	surgeon (the silent *e* preserves
falcon	soft *g*)

-an ||||||||||||||||||||||||||||||||||||||||||||||||||||||||||

The suffix *-an* is derived from Latin, meaning "belonging to," and is a familiar ending on words denoting places:

African	Californian	European
American	Cuban	Italian

It is also used to form other adjectives:

> human   Lutheran   urban   veteran

Two words in which **-an** is not a suffix:

> organ   orphan

47· -ate, -ite, AND -it

-ate and -ite ||||||||||||||||||||||||||||||||||||||||||||||||||||||

The Latin suffixes **-ate** and **-ite** cause no difficulty when they are stressed:

> appetite   dominate
> unite   ornate

But when they are not stressed, both sound alike and must be memorized.

Commonly occurring words with these endings are:

	-ate	*-ite*
accurate	fortunate	definite
adequate	legitimate	exquisite
chocolate	obstinate	favorite
climate	private	granite
desperate	senate	hypocrite
		opposite

Some of these words can be remembered by associating them with related forms in which the vowel is stressed:

> definite   defin*i*tion
> opposite   oppos*i*tion
> hypocrite   hypocr*i*tical

-it ||||||||||||||||||||||||||||||||||||||||||||||||||||||

A small group of words of various origins ends in **-it.** This ending is not a Latin suffix. Most of the words in this group have only two syllables, and, with one exception, they do not double the consonant after a short vowel:

bandit	habit
credit	merit
culprit	profit
deposit	

EXCEPTION: rabbit

48· -or, -er, AND -ar

-or and -er ||||||||||||||||||||||||||||||||||||||||||||||||||||||||||

The suffixes **-er** and **-or** sound alike because they are not stressed. The stress does not fall on these endings, but on an earlier syllable in the word. The suffix **-er** in **worker** sounds exactly the same as the **-or** in **sponsor.** The vowels, being unstressed, are not given their own distinct pronunciation.

The endings **-er** and **-or** not only sound alike, but they mean the same thing. A **worker** is one who works. A **survivor** is one who survives. Added to a root, **-er** and **-or** both mean "the one who." Sometimes, of course, they indicate a thing ("the one which") rather than a person:

accelerator	(accelerate)
distributor	(distribute)
elevator	(elevate)

Of the two endings, **-or** is somewhat more commonly used than **-er.** There is no easy way to remember which one to use. You will simply have to memorize each one individually and refer to your dictionary when in doubt.

Why do we have two endings that are spelled differently but mean the same thing? The answer, as usual, lies in the history of these words. It may not help you to remember the spelling of the words to know their history, but at least it will help you understand how it happened. The **-or** words are derived from a grammatical form of a Latin verb called the "perfect stem." For example, the word *assessor* comes from *assessus*, a "perfect" form of the verb *assidere*. Similarly, the word *inventor* comes from the Latin *inventus*, a "perfect" form of the verb *invenire.*

The ending *-er*, on the other hand, is used with root words derived from the present form rather than the perfect form of Latin verbs. The word *consumer*, for example, comes from *consumere*, a present rather than a perfect form. Likewise, *accuser* is derived from a present form in Latin.

The ending *-er* is also used with all root words of native English or non-Latin origin:

baker	helper	teacher
beginner	writer	worker

Even though the ending *-or* is found more often than *-er*, the tendency of a hesitant speller is usually to prefer the *-er* ending when in doubt. Perhaps this tendency occurs because the pronunciation seems to fit *-er* better than it does *-or*. Following is a checklist of common words ending in *-or* which are sometimes misspelled:

actor	creator	protector
administrator	distributor	separator
aggressor	doctor	spectator
author	educator	sponsor
bachelor	indicator	supervisor
collector	inspector	translator
commentator	investigator	visitor
competitor	operator	
conductor	professor	

Also, there seems to be a feeling that the *-or* ending is a bit more formal, professional, or scientific than the *-er* ending. Perhaps this feeling exists because so many *-er* words are native English, and therefore don't sound as "educated" as the words of Latin origin. When the word *realtor* was invented, it was obviously felt that *-or* looked more professional than *-er*. But when we make up everyday terms like *doubleheader* or *old-timer*, we instinctively use the less formal and more casual ending *-er*, which we associate in our minds with our everyday native English words.

Another example is the word **resistor,** used in electronics. We already had the word **resister,** which describes a person who resists. But the **-or** ending clearly looks more technical and scientific. From the word **resistor** we went on to create the word **transistor** by combining parts of **transfer** and **resistor.** A transistor transfers an electrical signal across a resistor.

-ar IIIIIIIIIIIIIIIIIIIIIIIIIIIIIIIIIIIIIIIIIIIIIIIIIIIIIIIIIIIIIIIIIIIIIIIIIIIIIIIIII

Only a very small group of words that mean "one who" uses the ending **-ar.** Below are the only ones you are apt to run into often:

beggar	registrar
liar	scholar

The ending **-ar** is also used to form adjectives, just like the ending **-al.** You recall how **spinal** is made by adding **-al** to **spine,** and **formal** by adding **-al** to **form.**

The suffix **-ar** is an alternative form of the ending **-al.** However, it is not used nearly as much. Below are the most common examples. Notice that in each word the letter *l* comes just before the ending. By using **-ar** instead of **-al,** the combination **-lal** is avoided, thus making the word easier to pronounce.

familiar	regular
particular	similar
peculiar	singular
popular	spectacular

In addition to the adjective **familiar,** we also have **familial.** **Familiar** means "closely acquainted," whereas **familial** means "having to do with the family."

Finally, we have a few nouns ending in **-ar** in which the **-ar** is not a suffix added to a root word. These words therefore do not mean "one who." They simply happen to end in **-ar.** They are mentioned here because they, too, are not stressed on the final syllable. They, too, have the neutral unstressed vowel and might easily be misspelled:

calendar	collar	grammar
cedar	dollar	vinegar

Although you may not have occasion to spell them very often, there are two words closely resembling *calendar* (a listing of the days and months of the year). These are:

calender, an industrial machine for rolling or pressing, and *colander,* a perforated kitchen utensil used for draining food.

Test yourself now over the following words drawn from the three preceding sections. Take the test before reviewing the lists below. Have someone pronounce the words for you as you write them, then correct your errors and review those sections which explain the correct spellings. Repeat until you can spell all the words without error. Remember that some of the following words contain problems of doubled consonants, some contain problems of unstressed vowels in the last syllables:

satin	cinnamon	definite	aggressor
raisin	determine	adequate	competitor
imagine	abandon	desperate	beggar
pigeon	aspirin	hypocrite	consumer
talon	orphan	accurate	collector
famine	patron	habit	scholar
origin	genuine	rabbit	similar

49·-ible AND -able

Section 27 has already introduced you to these unstressed endings that sound alike. Like **-er** and **-or,** they not only sound alike, but mean the same thing. And the reason for this similarity is also the same: both **-able** and **-ible** come from Latin. Originally **-able** was used with one class of verbs, while **-ible** was used with the others. Nowadays few people know Latin, and the difference has become meaningless.

A few practical hints can help you remember many of these words. If, for example, a hard *c* or *g* comes just before the ending, you know it will have to be *-able* rather than *-ible*. Otherwise the *c* would have an "s" sound and the *g* would be soft. The following words have *a* in the ending because *c* and *g* are hard:

applicable	indefatigable
practicable	navigable

If a soft *c* or *g* comes just before the ending, you know the suffix has to be *-ible*:

forcible	legible	negligible

Another simple test can also be applied. Remove the suffix (*-able* or *-ible*) and see what you have left. If the root word is complete in itself when the suffix is removed, then the ending is more likely to be *-able,* the reason being that *-able* is still a "live" suffix. It is used to form new words in English freely, whether they came originally from Latin or not. Therefore, if you take away the ending and have a familiar English root word, rather than a Latin root, your chances of being right are far greater if you spell the ending *-able.*

avail	available	regret	regrettable
depend	dependable	remark	remarkable
fashion	fashionable	tax	taxable
peace	peaceable	wash	washable
read	readable		

(Why is *regrettable* spelled with two *t*'s? Why didn't *peaceable* drop the *e* after *c*? If you can't remember, review Sections 15 and 30.)

When you remove the ending, you may also discover a root word whose final *-e* was dropped when *-able* was added:

blame	blamable	excite	excitable
dispose	disposable	presume	presumable

A third fact can help you remember many words whose roots are Latin. If the word has a noun form ending in *-ation,* the adjective ending will be **-able.** Both **-ation** and **-able** begin with *a*:

admiration	admirable
appreciation	appreciable
commendation	commendable
consideration	considerable
demonstration	demonstrable
estimation	estimable
inflammation	inflammable
irritation	irritable

If the noun form ends in **-ion** rather than **-ation,** the ending will be **-ible.** Both endings begin with *i*:

collection	collectible
comprehension	comprehensible
corruption	corruptible
exhaustion	exhaustible
digestion	digestible
perfection	perfectible
permission	permissible

EXCEPTION: correction — correctable

Finally, we have words which simply can't be classified in any of the groups above. Such words you will have to memorize, or check in your dictionary when you are uncertain. Below is a checklist of some you may frequently run across:

-able	*-ible*	
affable	audible	irresistible
culpable	collapsible	legible
equitable	contemptible	negligible
formidable	credible	possible
inevitable	flexible	responsible
insuperable	forcible	sensible
memorable	gullible	terrible
predictable	horrible	
sociable		
vulnerable		

A USEFUL HINT: Notice the difference between *-ble* and *-bly*:

possible	possibly
terrible	terribly
responsible	responsibly
probable	probably
inevitable	inevitably
peaceable	peaceably

Occasionally, someone writing in haste will make the mistake of writing *-ble* for *-bly*: "I could not possible go." This mistake is usually only an oversight, but it can be avoided. Any word ending in *-le* can be given an *-ly* ending simply by changing the *e* to *y*. Other examples:

simple	simply
ample	amply

Below is a selected list of *-able* and *-ible* words in scrambled order. Have someone read the words as you write them. Take the test before studying the list. Then review the ones you missed until you can spell all words correctly.

dependable	comprehensible	correctable
peaceable	forcible	horrible
collectible	memorable	negligible
regrettable	inevitable	sociable
irritable	legible	responsible
gullible	inflammable	admirable
credible	flexible	audible

50· -ent AND -ant; -ence AND -ance; -ency AND -ancy

You will not be surprised to find three more pairs of suffixes belonging to the same category as *-able* and *-ible, -er* and *-or*. These suffixes also come from Latin. Each pair of suffixes has two different spellings for the same meaning. Again the reason is to be found in the Latin language rather than in English. The *a* can be traced to one grammatical form in Latin, the *e* to another, and these spelling differences have been carried over into English. Several ways for remembering them are:

If an adjective form ends in **-ent,** the related noun will end in **-ence** or **-ency**; if **-ant,** then **-ance** or **-ancy**:

ADJECTIVE	NOUN
competent	competence
confident	confidence
dependent	dependence
different	difference
eminent	eminence
evident	evidence
excellent	excellence
innocent	innocence
insistent	insistence
permanent	permanence
persistent	persistence
prevalent	prevalence
prominent	prominence
violent	violence
decent	decency
potent	potency
urgent	urgency
abundant	abundance
brilliant	brilliance
elegant	elegance
ignorant	ignorance
important	importance
radiant	radiance
resistant	resistance
resonant	resonance
tolerant	tolerance
constant	constancy
infant	infancy
vacant	vacancy

Here is another way to remember whether to use *e* or *a* in the suffix: if a hard *g* or *c* comes just before it, the suffix begins with *a*. (An *e* would make the *c* or *g* soft.)

elegant	elegance
extravagant	extravagance
significant	significance

If a soft *g* or *c* comes just before it, the suffix begins with *e*.

decent	decency
intelligent	intelligence
magnificent	magnificence
urgent	urgency

One group of words always takes *-ent* or *-ence*: words like *occur*, *refer*, and *prefer*, which end in *r* and are usually stressed on that last syllable:

abhorrence	preference
conference	reference
occurrence	transference

Include also those which end in *-ere* (that is, a long *e* plus a silent *e*):

adhere	adherence
cohere	coherence
interfere	interference
revere	reverence

If neither of these two hints applies to a word, then you will have to rely on memory or on your dictionary. Below are lists of *-ence* and *-ance* words commonly used.

-ence ||||||||||||||||||||||||||||||||||||||||||||||||||||||||

The word most often misspelled:

existence

Words with *i* before *-ence* or before *-ent* (don't overlook the *i*):

audience	aud·i·ence
convenience	con·ve·ni·ence
experience	ex·per·i·ence
ingredient	in·gre·di·ent
conscience	con·sci·ence (in pronunciation, the last two letter groups are run together to form a single syllable)

Words with *u* before the **-ence:**

affluence	af·flu·ence
influence	in·flu·ence

Words with an unstressed vowel in the middle:

perm*a*nence
prev*a*lence (associate it with prev*a*il)

comp*e*tence (associate it with comp*e*te)
diff*e*rence
prec*e*dence (associate it with prec*e*de)

em*i*nence
ev*i*dence
prom*i*nence

Miscellaneous:

sentence
tendency

-ance IIIIIIIIIIIIIIIIIIIIIIIIIIIIIIIIIIIIIIIIIIIIIIIIIIIIIIIII

Most often misspelled:

abund*a*nce (*-ance,* not *-ence*)
brill*i*ance (notice the *i* before the *a*)
rad*i*ance (notice the *i* before the last *a*)
irrel*e*vance (watch the unstressed vowel)

Two special cases:

maintenance   sustenance

These two words are related to *maintain* and *sustain,* but are NOT formed by adding *-ance* to the verb forms. Both are derived from Old French words, *maintenir* and *sustenir. Maintenance* and *sustenance* have preserved the *e* in the middle syllable. Therefore, we have

maintain	BUT:	maintenance
sustain	BUT:	sustenance

Other words ending in *-ance* for which there is no special rule:

acceptance	continuance
acquaintance	entrance
admittance	guidance
appearance	performance
assistance	remembrance
attendance	vengeance

The word *apparent* often confuses a hesitant speller because it somewhat resembles the word *appearance* in both pronunciation and meaning. But notice that *apparent* does not have the word *appear* in it. Keep the two separate in your mind.

-ent and -ant |||||||||||||||||||||||||||||||||||||||||||||||||||||||||||||||||||

Just above, you saw that *-ent* and *-ant* are the most commonly used suffixes to form adjectives. Many of these adjectives have related nouns ending in *-ence* or *-ency, -ance* or *-ancy.* Somewhat less often, *-ent* and *-ant* are used to form nouns. In such cases, the suffix forms a word meaning "the one who," or "the thing which."

-ent		*-ant*	
adherent	incident	claimant	pageant
agent	solvent	defendant	servant
antecedent	superintendent	inhabitant	tenant
dependent		litigant	variant

Notice that the legal terms—*defendant, litigant, claimant*—all end in *-ant.* This may help you remember how to spell *warrant,* a native English word not derived from Latin, but which happens to end in *-ant* like the other legal terms.

(Why does *pageant* have a silent *e* after the *g*?)

Watch out for this common confusion:

> dominant (don't confuse with the verb *dominate*)
> predominant

Below are selected words to use as a test. See how many you can spell correctly before you study them. You can also use the word lists in the preceding section for additional practice testing.

magnificence	convenience	reverence
dependence	occurrence	coherent
maintenance	pageant	prevalence
existence	assistance	precedence
evident	different	brilliant
prominent	eminent	defendant
irrelevant	experience	warrant
permanent	influence	appearance
guidance	inhabitant	apparent

51· -ery AND -ary

These two suffixes are different from the preceding ones: fortunately, they *don't* both mean the same thing. This difference will help you to keep them apart in your mind. In fact, only a very few words are ever misspelled because of confusion between these two endings. Yet these few words often appear on spelling lists and tests.

-ery ||||||||||||||||||||||||||||||||||||||||||||||||||||||||||||

The suffix *-ery* denotes a place of business, where something is manufactured, produced, or sold:

bakery	grocery
confectionery	hatchery
creamery	millinery
distillery	winery
fishery	

-ery also denotes a place where certain things are done:

cemetery   monastery

The word **stationery** (writing paper) can be more easily re-membered if you associate it, too, with a place of business. **Stationery** is sold in a stationery store; the same group of words includes **grocery**, **bakery**, and **creamery**. You can also apply a simple memory device: a **letter** is written on **stationery**. Both words have **er** in them.

A thing that stands still is **stationary**. It is "stationed," or "static." **Stationary** is an adjective, like **revolutionary** or **budgetary**.

Other nouns ending in *-ery*, besides those meaning places of business, are very seldom misspelled. Here are some of the more common ones:

bravery	forgery	pottery
cookery	gallery	slavery
finery	lottery	snobbery

The one-syllable roots of most of these words are obvious: **brave**, **forge**, **lot**, **pot**, **cook**, **fine**, **snob**, and **slave**.

One word of Greek origin is sometimes difficult to remember:

dysentery

The first syllable, **dys-**, is spelled with a **y**. In Greek, **dys** meant "bad" or "difficult." It is not the same as our prefix **dis-**, which is very commonly used to mean "not" or "opposite to"—as in **disadvantage** and **disabled**. The second syllable contains a neutral, unstressed vowel whose spelling can't be identified by its pronunciation. And the ending *-ery* doesn't fit any of the above classifications. The Greek word for "intestine" was **enteron**. **Dysentery** therefore means literally "bad intestine." Knowing the origin of an unusual word will help you remember it.

-ary ||||||||||||||||||||||||||||||||||||||||||||||||||||||||||||

Words ending in *-ary* seldom cause a spelling problem. This ending, like *-ar*, is used to create adjectives:

coronary	honorary	salutary
customary	military	secondary
disciplinary	monetary	solitary
elementary	rotary	stationary

It is also used to create nouns:

anniversary	dictionary	mortuary
boundary	dignitary	sanctuary
capillary	functionary	secretary
diary	library	vocabulary

Below is a scrambled list of *-ary* and *-ery* words from this section. Only the root of each word is given. Finish each word by adding either *-ary* or *-ery*. Check your answers against the word lists in this section.

element	monast	hatch
secret	solit	sanctu
vocabul	annivers	station (writing paper)
dysent	slav	station (standing still)

52· -ceed, -cede, AND -sede

The three spellings *-ceed*, *-cede*, and *-sede* are all regular ways of spelling the same sound. Only twelve words in the English language end in these syllables.

Only one ends in *-sede*:

supersede

Only three end in *-ceed*:

exceed
proceed
succeed

The remaining eight end in *-cede*:

accede	cede	intercede	recede
antecede	concede	precede	secede

Two pairs of these words seem to be the source of most of the confusion surrounding this group of spellings:

precede	secede
proceed	succeed

Proceed means "to continue along a course of action."
Precede means "to go before or in advance."
Succeed means either "to follow after" or "to attain a goal—to be successful."
Secede means "to withdraw."
There is no good reason why three words should be spelled **-ceed** instead of **-cede** like the majority. The root of both **-cede** and **-ceed** is the Latin verb **cedere,** "to go." This root explains why the word **procedure** is spelled with a single **e** between **c** and **d,** rather than **ee** like the related word **proceed. Procedure** is closer to the spelling of the root, **-cede,** than is **proceed,** and is therefore more regular.
The **s** in **supersede** has a reasonable explanation. The root **sede** is not the same word as **cede.** It comes from the Latin **sedere,** "to sit," rather than **cedere,** "to go." From **sedere** we also get **sediment** and **sedentary.**

Without looking back, test yourself by answering the following questions:
What is the only word ending in **-sede?**
What are the only three words ending in **-ceed?**
What is the difference in meaning between **proceed** and **precede,** and between **succeed** and **secede?**

53· -ize AND -ise

The ending **-ise** is preferred in British spelling, whereas **-ize** is preferred in the United States. In neither country is there any complete agreement on how to spell every word with this ending. Therefore you may find a word spelled sometimes one way, sometimes another.

Always spell the following words with *-ise,* NEVER with *-ize*:

advertise	despise	franchise	advise
chastise	disguise	merchandise	devise
comprise	enterprise	surmise	improvise
compromise	excise	surprise	revise
demise	exercise		supervise

If they end in *-vise,* as they do in the last column, they will always be spelled with *s* rather than *z.*

DON'T let the ghost of *prize* haunt you in **surprise.**

Only two common words end in *-yze*:

analyze   paralyze

Spell all others *-ize.* Examples:

apologize	baptize	criticize	realize
authorize	capitalize	organize	recognize

The ending *-ize* is widely used to create new verbs, like **normalize** and **hospitalize.** You will readily recognize the root word in such cases.

Another tip: A few root words, like **rise** and **wise,** are used to make compounds like **moonrise** and **likewise.** These words are not cases of an *-ise* suffix.

54· -ly AND -ally; -acle AND -icle

You have already met the suffix *-ly* and have learned that it is commonly added to a root word without causing any change in the spelling of that root. No letters are dropped or added:

final	finally	loud	loudly
free	freely	slow	slowly

In Section 36, you were introduced to the group of adjectives ending in *-ic.* This suffix means "characterized by." Here are some nouns with their adjective forms ending in *-ic*:

artist	artistic	fantasy	fantastic
base	basic	academy	academic

The ending *-ally* rather than *-ly* is added to such words to form an adverb:

academically	emphatically
artistically	fantastically
automatically	frantically
basically	scientifically
drastically	terrifically

There is a reason for this. Along with the suffix *-ic* is another similar suffix, *-ical,* also used to form adjectives:

clerical	inimical	practical
geological	logical	radical
grammatical	physical	symmetrical

When *-ly* is added to these words, they all end in *-ically*:

radically	symmetrically	geologically

Some adjectives, then, end in *-ic* and others in *-ical.* But in order to give their adverb forms all the same ending (*-ically*), *-ally* is added to words ending only in *-ic.* Thus we get *scientifically* from *scientific* to match *geologically* from *geological.*

There is only one EXCEPTION:

publicly

Accidentally and *coincidentally* are formed from *accidental* and *coincidental.* Don't leave out *al.*

A small group of words has the endings *-acle* or *-icle,* which sound alike.

barnacle	article
manacle	bicycle
miracle	chronicle
oracle	cuticle
pinnacle	icicle
receptacle	particle
tentacle	vehicle

Lincoln Christian College

Monocle has *o* in the ending instead of *a* or *i* because it is derived from the Latin *monoculus,* "one-eyed."

Now test yourself by adding either *-ly* or *-ally* to the following words:

basic	terrific	drastic
logical	practical	automatic
public	physical	scientific

55· -efy AND -ify

Only four words in common usage end in *-efy*:

liquefy   putrefy   rarefy   stupefy

Even *liquefy* is more and more often being spelled *liquify,* because of its similarity to the word *liquid.* The dictionary recognizes this spelling as acceptable. All others end in *-ify.* Examples:

testify   horrify   classify   justify

Why do a few words have an *e* where most have *i*? The explanation lies in their Latin roots. The Latin roots of the four exceptions above are:

| liquefy | putrefy | rarefy | stupefy |
| liquefacere | putrefacere | rarefacere | stupefacere |

None of the words ending in *-ify* can be traced to Latin roots whose *e* is carried over into English. Many of them, such as *beautify, mystify, typify,* and *classify,* have no original Latin form at all but were created later, even though the root words (*beauty, mystery, type,* and *class*) can be traced back to Latin.

Sometimes the suffix *-ify* is even added to root words that did not originate in Latin:

dandy   dandify

A useful tip: There is no suffix "*-afy.*"

56· WORDS ENDING IN -ous

Like most suffixes, **-ous** too is unstressed. Its vowel sound comes out neutral, like "us." It means "full of":

joy   joyous (full of joy)

It follows the same regular pattern of any suffix that begins with a vowel. If the last letter in the root word is a consonant, there is no change in spelling:

bulb	bulbous
humor	humorous
poison	poisonous
prosper	prosperous
riot	riotous

SOME EXCEPTIONS:

disastrous   fibrous   wondrous

When **-ous** is added to the root words—**disaster, fiber,** and **wonder**—the **e** is dropped.

If the root word ends in a consonant plus **y,** the **y** is changed to an **i:**

glory	glorious
luxury	luxurious

If the root word ends in a vowel plus **y,** the **y** is kept:

joy   joyous

If the root word ends in a silent **e,** the **e** is dropped:

fame   famous

If the root word ends in a soft **g,** the **e** is kept in order to preserve the soft sound:

advantage	advantageous
courage	courageous
outrage	outrageous

So far, the suffix **-ous** offers no problems. It is easy to recognize the root word and the regular addition of **-ous.**

But as you have noticed before, there is a group of words whose roots remain buried in history. We can no longer separate a familiar root from its ending:

> curious (Latin *cura,* meaning "care")
> generous (Latin *genus,* "race or kind," implying nobility)
> tedious (Latin *taedium,* "weariness")

Such words offer a spelling problem in the letters that come just before the **-ous** ending. First of all, there is a group of words in which a vowel precedes the **-ous** ending:

amphibious	am·phib·i·ous
bounteous	boun·te·ous
contemporaneous	con·tem·por·a·ne·ous
courteous	cour·te·ous
curious	cur·i·ous
hideous	hid·e·ous
spontaneous	spon·ta·ne·ous
tedious	te·di·ous
vitreous	vit·re·ous

If you are a hesitant speller, it is easy to overlook the *i* or *e* that precedes the suffix, or to fail to put it in its right place. Students have been known to misspell **curious** as "*curouis,*" or "*couris,*" or "*curoius.*" This mistake occurs because they don't know exactly where to put the several vowel letters. Remember that the ending is **-ous,** and that an unstressed vowel comes just before it. Pronounce the words syllable by syllable as they are shown above, noting how each syllable in the root is spelled (most of them are regular), and how an *i* or an *e* fits in just before the **-ous** ending.

There is no rule for remembering whether to use an *i* or an *e* in such words. The history of each word would explain how the vowel got there, but this history would not help you remember it.

Second, you may have a spelling problem with **-ous** words which have a "sh" sound just before the ending:

precious   ambitious   conscious

These words are pronounced "preshəs," "ambishəs," "conshəs," which means that you can't spell them by ear. Begin by separating out the *-ous* ending and the syllables at the beginning:

ambitious	ambi(ti)ous
conscious	con(sci)ous
precious	pre(ci)ous

This separation leaves you only with the problem of spelling the "sh" sound between the beginning and ending syllables. And even this problem is easier than you may think. The different ways of spelling the "sh" sound are explained below.

-scious |||||||||||||||||||||||||||||||||||||||||||||||||||||||

Only two words end in *-scious*: *conscious* and *luscious*. The root portion of *conscious*, *-sci-*, comes from the Latin verb *scire*, meaning "to know." It enters into several other words, such as *science, conscience, omniscience,* and *omniscient.* The other rarity, *luscious,* is believed to be a blend of *lush* and *delicious,* with the *s* from the one word and the *ci* from the other.

-tious |||||||||||||||||||||||||||||||||||||||||||||||||||||||

An adjective with this ending normally has a corresponding noun that ends in *-tion*:

ambitious	ambition
cautious	caution
contentious	contention
expeditious	expedition
fictitious	fiction

A few, like *facetious* (humorous), *factitious* (artificial), *bumptious* (aggressive), or *conscientious* (painstaking), do not have corresponding nouns.

-cious ||||||||||||||||||||||||||||||||||||||||||||||||||||||||||

Most other *-ous* words preceded by the "sh" sound end in *-cious*:

delicious	precious
ferocious	spacious
gracious	vicious

Odds and Ends |||||||||||||||||||||||||||||||||||||||||||||||||||||||||||||||||||||||||

Here are a few **-ous** words with peculiarities that don't fit into any of the groups that have been described:

anxious	nauseous
gorgeous	religious
herbaceous	righteous

In each case, the vowel just before the suffix has been absorbed into a single sound with the foregoing consonant: "ch" (*right-eous*), "sh" (*anxious, nauseous, herbaceous*), and soft *g* (*gorgeous, religious*).

The word **miscellaneous** troubles some people, but the problem lies in the *sc* and the double *l* more than in the **-eous** ending.

The two words **piteous** and **plenteous** look as if they ought to have an *i* instead of an *e* before the **-ous** ending, because of the root words **pity** and **plenty.** But both have a very long history, and the *e* goes back to an early spelling which is still retained.

Next, we have words with a vowel other than *e* or *i* before the suffix:

-uous |||||||||||||||||||||||||||||||||||||||||||||||||||||||||||||||||||||||||

This suffix is different in Latin from the simple **-ous** ending. It means "tending to" rather than "full of." But the only important thing to remember here is that many words end in **-uous** as well as in **-ious** and **-eous.** Since the long *u* is always pronounced, these words can usually be spelled by ear:

ambiguous	am·big·u·ous
assiduous	as·sid·u·ous
conspicuous	con·spic·u·ous
continuous	con·tin·u·ous
deciduous	de·cid·u·ous
perspicuous	per·spic·u·ous

presumptuous	pre·sump·tu·ous
sensuous	sen·su·ous
tortuous	tor·tu·ous
vacuous	vac·u·ous

Notice that **tortuous** has no **r** before the ending. It is not *"tor-turous,"* but **tortuous.** Its root meaning is "to twist" or "to turn." The word **torture** comes from the same root originally, but it now no longer refers only to methods of twisting or turning. A tortuous road is filled with many turns and bends—not necessarily one which tortures the driver.

You might misplace the **u** in these words if your eye becomes confused by seeing another **u** so close by in the **-ous** ending. But you can keep the vowels straight by careful separation of the words into syllables.

A very small group of words ends in **-us.** These are all nouns borrowed directly from Latin. The large group of **-ous** words, on the other hand, are all adjectives.

bonus	circus
campus	focus
calculus	hocus-pocus
census	radius

Hocus-pocus is apparently imitation Latin, invented by jugglers and magicians.

-ose ||||||||||||||||||||||||||||||||||||||||||||||||||||||||

Finally, there are a few words ending in **-ose,** which is another version of **-ous,** or "full of." These words offer no spelling problem, since they are spelled regularly just as they are pronounced:

| grandiose | comatose |
| verbose | globose |

Below are two tests. First, change the following words to their **-ous** forms. The correct spellings can be found in the word lists of this section.

Examples: ambition   ambitious
            joy   joyous

advantage   continue   space
caution   religion   luxury
glory   outrage   courtesy

Second, have someone read the following words while you write them. Then review the ones you missed by going back to the explanations of the correct spelling in this section. Repeat the test until you can remember each word correctly.

curious	precious	sensuous
hideous	vicious	tortuous
fictitious	anxious	gorgeous
conscious	luscious	righteous
conspicuous	delicious	plenteous

57· WORDS ENDING IN -ion

Of all the hundreds of words ending in *-ion,* most end in either *-sion* or *-tion.* Since these endings are usually pronounced exactly alike—as if spelled "shun"—the problem is simply whether to use an *s* or a *t.*

One thing is certain: the "sh" in these words is almost never spelled with the letters *sh.* The words *cushion* and *fashion* are the only common words ending in *-shion* rather than in *-sion* or *-tion.*

Like so many others, the *-ion* words fall into groups that make the spelling much easier to remember.

-tion |||!||||||||||||||||||||||||||||||||||||||||||||||||||||||||||||||

First, there is a large group of words which are always spelled with the *-tion* ending. These are words in which a long vowel comes just before the ending and the ending is pronounced "shun," with the soft, or unvoiced, consonant sound "sh":

completion   dil*u*tion   nation
dev*o*tion   lotion   sol*u*tion

This regularity means that all the hundreds of words ending in *-ation* will be spelled with *-tion* rather than *-sion*:

discrimination	integration	realization
domination	medication	relation
education	nomination	simplification
elimination	qualification	standardization

It may help reinforce your memory to know that most of the verbs ending in *-ate, -fy,* or *-ize* form nouns ending in *-ation*:

regulate	regulation
classify	classification
civilize	civilization

Many other *-tion* words can be remembered by associating them with related words. For example, if *t* comes at the end of the root word, the ending *-tion* will always be used:

act	action	elect	election
adopt	adoption	erupt	eruption
connect	connection	ignite	ignition
discrete	discretion	prevent	prevention
distort	distortion		

We can add *portion* to this list, since it is related to the word *part.*

-sion ||||||||||||||||||||||||||||||||||||||||||||||||||||||||||||||||

Second, there is a group of words always spelled with the ending *-sion.* In these words the *s* is pronounced with the hard, or voiced, sound "zh," as in *vision* and *confusion.* Say the following words out loud:

VOICED	UNVOICED
explosion	lotion

Pronunciation: "ex·plo·zhun" "lo·shun"

All words which are pronounced with the voiced sound "zh" are spelled with the ending **-sion**:

conclusion	explosion	precision
confusion	fusion	profusion
cohesion	invasion	revision
division	intrusion	version
evasion	lesion	vision
excision	occasion	

EXCEPTION: Only one single common word with the voiced "zh" sound is spelled with the **-tion** ending:

equation

The word **occasion** is the only one on the above list very often misspelled. This error occurs because a hesitant speller doesn't know whether to double the **c** or the **s**, or both. The **c** is doubled because of assimilation of the Latin prefix **ob-** (see Section 31 on prefixes). But **ss** is never pronounced "zh." Besides, the double **s** would require the preceding vowel to be short rather than long: "*occassion*" would rhyme with *passion*. **Occasion** must be spelled with one **s**, like **invasion** and **evasion**.

The great mass of **-ion** words are therefore reduced to only a few which need cause any hesitation in spelling. Let us take a closer look at the ones that are left. In the two groups below, notice the consonant that comes just before the ending:

-sion		*-tion*	
compulsion	expansion	caption	attention
emulsion	extension	fraction	convention
revulsion	mansion	junction	mention
	pension	production	retention
comprehension	pretension	sanction	
dimension	tension	section	

The consonants **n** and **l** are the only ones appearing before **-sion** when it has the unvoiced pronunciation "shun." Only where **n** appears before the ending is there any overlap. Notice that several of the **-sion** words are formed from verbs ending in a **d** which converts to an **s**:

comprehend	comprehension
expand	expansion
extend	extension
pretend	pretension

This grouping leaves less than a dozen common words which might possibly be spelled with either **-sion** or **-tion.** Review the columns above before taking the test at the end of this section.

-ssion ||||||||||||||||||||||||||||||||||||||||||||||||||||||||

Next, there are words that have the ending **-ssion,** instead of **-sion** or **-tion.** There are not very many of this kind, and again there are several simple ways to remember most of them.

Some are formed from verbs which end in **-ss:**

compress	compression
digress	digression
express	expression
possess	possession
regress	regression
repress	repression
suppress	suppression

Some are formed from verbs ending in **-it:**

submit	submission
omit	omission
permit	permission

The word **mission** is not hard to remember, and it appears as a part of each of the three words above. In fact, it is derived from the same Latin root. Another common word from this source is **intermission.**

Only a few other common words end in **-ssion:**

passion　　　compassion　　　fission

In every case, the double **s** is preceded by a short vowel, according to the regular pattern you have already learned. You know there cannot be a double **s** following a long vowel.

-cion ||||||||||||||||||||||||||||||||||||||||||||||||||||||||

Finally, a very few words use **c** instead of **t** or **s** in the ending. Always bear in mind that the vast majority of **-ion** words end in either *-tion* or *-sion,* and that pronunciation can usually guide you in which to use. The ending *-ssion* is used for only a few, and the ending *-cion* for hardly any at all:

coercion   suspicion

A hesitant speller may imagine that the *-cion* ending is common simply because many words end in *-cious* or *-cial*: *delicious, precious, special,* or *commercial.* But remember that *-cion* is actually rare.

Oddities ||||||||||||||||||||||||||||||||||||||||||||||||||||||||||||

One common word uses *x*:

complexion

This word is often misspelled *"complection."* But *complexion* is related to the word *complex,* even though the meanings of the two words no longer seem to be connected.

Another word is in a class by itself:

ocean

This, of course, is not a form of the *-ion* ending at all, but is derived from the Latin *oceanus* and has developed the pronunciation "o-shun" more or less accidentally.

Change the following words to a form ending in *-sion, -tion,* or *-ssion.* They are all taken from the word lists in Section 57.

Examples:	relate	relation
	elect	election
	compress	compression
	expand	expansion

explode	erupt	submit	revise
complete	conclude	coerce	educate
eliminate	extend	classify	prevent
divide	possess	intrude	omit
standardize	adopt	regulate	comprehend
connect	revise	express	confuse

Test yourself once more by having someone read the following words as you write them:

occasion	mansion	suspicion
devotion	mention	ocean
compulsion	complexion	permission
equation	realization	precision

58· WORDS ENDING IN -ure

The suffix *-ure* seldom causes a spelling problem, although it does sometimes cause momentary doubt or hesitation because it appears to have an irregular pronunciation. For example, read the two following words out loud:

teacher   creature

How does it happen that *-ture* sounds almost exactly like *-cher*?

The reason is not hard to understand. If *-ure* were stressed, it would sound as it does in the words *pure* or *cure.* But since as a suffix it is not stressed, it is rapidly pronounced "yər" instead, and the preceding *t* blends with the "y" sound to produce "chər." Therefore, *creature* and *feature* sound as if they might be spelled *"creacher"* or *"feacher."*

The majority of words ending in *-ure* follow the same pattern:

adventure	lecture	posture
capture	literature	puncture
conjecture	mixture	rupture
culture	moisture	structure
departure	nature	temperature
furniture	picture	torture

In similar fashion, *s* blends with *-ure* to form the sound "zh":

closure	measure
composure	pleasure
exposure	treasure
leisure	

Only two common words with this sound are spelled with a *z*:

seizure   azure

Likewise, *d* blends with *-ure* to form a "j" sound:

verdure   procedure

Only a few words have a double *s*:

fissure   pressure

Compare these words that have an unvoiced "sh" sound, spelled with *ss,* with the words above that have a voiced "zh" sound. The voiced sound is spelled with a single *s*: *closure, treasure.*

If a consonant comes before the *s,* the *s* always remains single; it is never doubled:

censure   tonsure

The words *censor* and *censure* are confusing because they are so much alike. *Censor* is the more familiar and also the stronger. It means "to suppress or ban something considered objectionable." *Censure* is a milder word that means "to express disapproval, blame, or criticism against something."

When consonants other than *t, d,* or *s* come before *-ure,* there is no seeming irregularity at all, for they do *not* blend with the long *u* and are spelled just as they are pronounced:

conjure   injure
failure   tenure
figure

59· A REVIEW OF WORDS WITH i OR e IN THE SUFFIX

You have seen how the letter *i* becomes absorbed by *c* and *s* and *t* in pronunciation to form a "sh" or "zh" sound:

appreciate	aggression	completion
crucial	ancient	devotion
efficient	cohesion	essential
especially	compassion	initiative
ferocious	occasion	invention
politician	omission	partial
precious	revision	penitentiary
special	session	relation
		substantial

It is also absorbed by the soft **g**:

allegiance	legion
contagion	religion

After **l** and **n**, it forms a "y" sound:

battalion	Californian
brilliant	companion
peculiar	petunia
valiant	spaniel

It forms a "y" sound also in **behavior.**

NOTE: The word **similar** is often misspelled "*similiar.*" It cannot end in **-iar**, or it would rhyme with *familiar.*

Such spellings are often bothersome to the hesitant speller, for the *i* seems to disappear in pronunciation. As you become more confident in spelling, you will develop the habit of seeing word-endings quickly: **-ial, -ian, -iar, -ion, -ious.** You will take the *i* for granted and be much less likely to leave it out by mistake—or to put it in where it does not belong.

Elsewhere, *i* is easier to keep track of, for it is pronounced as a separate syllable:

alien	jovial	radium
appropriate	lenient	radius
comedian	mania	soviet
custodian	medium	
dubious	radiant	

(A few of the above words are pronounced by some speakers with a "y" sound: "ale·yǝn," "doob·yǝs," "jove·yǝl," "leen·yǝnt.")

The letter *e* occurs in this position less frequently, and therefore causes less trouble:

spontaneous petroleum meteor

60· WORDS ENDING IN -y, -ey, AND -ie

The endings *-y, -ey,* and *-ie* often sound exactly alike in pronunciation. (Reread Section 21, p. 30, on the letter **y** to review the pronunciation of this extremely common unstressed ending.) However, the three spellings are very seldom confused with each other, because each one has its logical reason for being used.

First, remember that these three ending sound alike only when they are *not* stressed. When they are stressed in pronunciation, the stressed endings no longer sound the same as the unstressed endings:

STRESSED	UNSTRESSED
apply	faculty
deny	mystery
sky	rainy
obey	honey
survey	journey
they	trolley
die	caddie
lie	cutie
tie	toughie

-ey ||||||||||||||||||||||||||||||||||||||||||||||||||||||||||

Of these endings, *-ey* is the least common. Only about twenty-five or thirty common words end in unstressed *-ey.* And of these thirty, only a few ever seem to be misspelled because of the ending. Some *-ey* words you will frequently run across are:

alley	money
attorney	monkey
chimney	pulley
donkey	valley

In all the words above, the ending *-ey* is not a suffix. It has not been added to a root word. It is a part of the root word and can't be removed.

-y ||||||||||||||||||||||||||||||||||||||||||||||||||||||||||

The letter **y**, on the other hand, is often used as a suffix. It is used to form nouns:

entreaty	laundry
flattery	lethargy
inquiry	

Even more often **y** is used to form adjectives:

creamy	funny	sticky
curly	muddy	watery
dirty	sleepy	windy

The root words in all these examples are obvious: ***cream, mud, stick, fun,*** and so on.

It is possible for **-y** to be added to a word which already ends in **y**, such as ***sky*** or ***clay.*** But if you added **-y** alone, you would get *"skyy"* and *"clayy."* It would look like a double **y**, which is a combination never used in English. To avoid this combination, we use the ending **-ey** instead:

skyey   clayey

Words that end in **o** would also be confusing if **-y** alone were added: ***mosquito***—*"mosquitoy,"* ***tomato***—*"tomatoy."* The final syllable looks like the word ***toy.*** To avoid this combination, the ending **-ey** is used:

mosquitoey   tomatoey

Another exception is the word **holey,** meaning "full of holes." As you remember from Section 13, the final **e** of long-vowel words like **hole** is dropped when a suffix beginning with a vowel is added:

craze	crazy
flake	flaky
smoke	smoky

But if the **e** of **hole** were dropped, the spelling would be **holy,** which is already a word with an entirely different meaning. To avoid confusion, the word **holey** retains the **e** to denote the idea of a hole rather than sacredness.

-ie ||||||||||||||||||||||||||||||||||||||||||||||||||||||

The ending **-ie** is attached to words to imply something little or dear:

dearie	nightie	bootie

Or it may be attached to words to mean one of a certain kind. The resulting words are often slang expressions:

smartie	toughie	bookie

Since this suffix probably came from a Scottish dialect, it is not surprising to find some of the terms used in golf also ending in **-ie,** for golf originated in Scotland:

caddie	birdie	stymie

61· ADDING -s TO WORDS THAT END IN -y

If the final **y** is preceded by a vowel, simply add **-s.** No letters are dropped or changed:

alloy	alloys	play	plays
attorney	attorneys	portray	portrays
guy	guys	obey	obeys

But if the **y** is preceded by a consonant, change the **y** to **i** and add **-es** instead of just **-s:**

faculty	faculties	accompany	accompanies
industry	fantasies	apply	applies
industry	industries	carry	carries
sky	skies	study	studies
story	stories	try	tries
theory	theories	vary	varies

62· ADDING OTHER SUFFIXES TO WORDS THAT END IN -y

If the final **y** is preceded by a vowel, the **y** remains the same no matter what the suffix is:

| enjoy | enjoying | enjoyment |
| play | playing | playful |

If the final **y** is preceded by a consonant, the **y** changes to an **i**:

accompany	accompaniment	defy	defiant
beauty	beautiful	happy	happiness
busy	business	marry	marriage
carry	carriage	vary	various

EXCEPTION:

| lady | ladylike |

However, if the suffix begins with an **i**, the **y** is kept, so that two **i**'s will not come together:

apply	applying	defy	defying
carry	carrying	forty	fortyish
copy	copyist	study	studying

A few one-syllable words are somewhat irregular. In **shy, dry, sly,** and **spry,** the **y** does not change to an **i** before **-ly** and **-ness** even though it is preceded by a consonant:

| dryly | slyly | dryness | slyness |
| shyly | spryly | shyness | spryness |

But the **y** shifts to an **i** before other suffixes added to these one-syllable words just as in other words:

drier	slier	driest	sliest
shier	sprier	shiest	spriest

NOTE: You may occasionally find people spelling the above words with a *y*:

dryer	slyer	dryest	slyest
shyer	spryer	shyest	spryest

These spellings are not considered wrong, but are less often used than the regular forms.

Because a very few words are irregular and do retain the *y* before *-ly* and *-ness* when it would normally shift to *i*, doubt enters some people's minds whenever they face adding a suffix to any one-syllable word ending in *-y*. For example, many verbs are one-syllable words ending in a *-y* preceded by a consonant:

cry	fly	spy
dry	ply	try

The *y* changes to *i*, and *-es* is added:

cries	flies	spies
dries	plies	tries

These verbs follow the regular pattern. They are never spelled *"crys," "drys,"* and so on.

REMEMBER: Only when *-ly* or *-ness* is added to a one-syllable word ending in *-y* is the *y* retained. Otherwise, these words follow the same rules as all other words ending in *-y*.

63· ADDING -s TO WORDS THAT END IN -o

If the final *o* is preceded by a vowel, always add *-s* (never *-es*):

duo	duos	radio	radios
embryo	embryos	studio	studios
folio	folios	tattoo	tattoos
igloo	igloos	zoo	zoos

If a consonant precedes the final *o,* the ending for a few common words is always *-es*:

echo	echoes	potato	potatoes
embargo	embargoes	tomato	tomatoes
hero	heroes	torpedo	torpedoes
Negro	Negroes		

But most of the time you will be safe in simply adding *-s* to words whose final *o* is preceded by a consonant. For example, all musical terms add only *-s*:

altos	solos
concertos	sopranos
pianos	

Other words that regularly add only *-s* are:

dynamo	dynamos	silo	silos
ego	egos	tobacco	tobaccos
photo	photos	two	twos

What confuses the hesitant speller is the fact that many words can take either *-s* or *-es.* The following words are correctly spelled either way:

banjos	banjoes	mottos	mottoes
buffalos	buffaloes	tornados	tornadoes
cargos	cargoes	zeros	zeroes
dominos	dominoes		

How can you remember, then, which ending to use? The answer is simple: memorize the few words that always end in *-es,* and use *-s* for all the others. Your chances of being correct are far greater if you use *-s* rather than *-es* for most words. If you are unsure, look up the correct spelling in your dictionary. If *-es* is the required ending, your dictionary will say so. If it says nothing, then *s* is the correct plural.

Remember, too, that one-syllable words, like **hoe** and **toe,** are almost the only ones that end in *-oe* in the singular. Words of more than one syllable, like **potato** and **tomato,** almost invariably end in **-o** in the singular. Virtually the only exception is *oboe.*

Now test yourself by adding endings to the following words. You can find the correct answers in Sections 60–63.

Add **-y** to these words:

fun	mosquito	hole
water	smoke	inquire

Add **-s** to these words:

beauty	enjoy	bookie	dry	spy
embryo	zoo	echo	tomato	photo
soprano	motto	attorney	buffalo	hero

Add the suffix **-age**:

marry	carry

Add the suffix **-ness**:

happy	shy	dry

Add the suffix **-ful**:

beauty	play

64· OTHER WORDS THAT END IN VOWELS

Most English words end in a consonant sound. Only a minority of words end in an open-vowel sound, such as the **y** you have just studied in words like *party* and *democracy.*

Another short vowel that sometimes comes at the end of words is the **a** in many proper names like *America, Alaska, California, Canada, Martha,* and *Linda.* It is also found at the end of some common nouns, mostly borrowed from foreign languages:

camera	idea	saliva
comma	parka	soda

The most common open vowels at the end of words are the long ones, which are usually spelled with digraphs:

a	e	i	o	u
delay	sea	die	toe	argue
pay	agree	tie	grow	continue
portray	committee		bungalow	curfew
obey	Tennessee		tomorrow	

Long *i* is not usually spelled with a digraph at the end of a word. It is more often spelled with a **y**:

deny	satisfy
reply	try

It appears as a single *i* in only a very few foreign borrowings:

alkali	alibi	rabbi

Long *o* can appear as a single *o*:

also	jumbo
go	tomato
hero	

However, long *a* never appears at the end of words as a single letter *a*; it is always a digraph: *betray, survey.*

Long *u* appears as the single letter *u* in only a few foreign borrowings:

emu	menu
impromptu	Peru

Long *e* appears as the single letter *e* in a few borrowed words:

aborigine	apostrophe	facsimile
acme	catastrophe	posse
acne	epitome	recipe

This last group is the only one that causes the hesitant speller any real difficulty, for the simple reason that the ending sounds exactly like the common -*y* ending, as in *enemy, Emily, bossy,* or *canopy.* The only way to master this group is to familiarize yourself with the few words ending in *e* that are very commonly used.

Finally, there is the minor but sometimes bothersome problem of adding suffixes to words that end in **-ue.** The rule to follow is: drop the **e** in most cases:

argue	arguing	imbue	imbuing
	argument	rescue	rescuing
	arguable	statue	statuary
continue	continuing	true	truly
due	duly	value	valuable

BUT: valueless

PART III

Variations in Vowels and Consonants

The glory and horror of English spelling is that it so often gives you a choice of more than one way to spell the same sound. Now that you have learned the most common and expected spellings, you are ready for the minor variations and alternatives. These variations occur mostly in small groups of words that follow consistent principles within themselves. They might be called "regular irregularities."

65· THE DIGRAPHS ie AND ei

You will have no trouble recognizing the *regular* spellings in which the letters *ie* and *ei* come together:

alien	hierarchy	agreeing
copier	quiet	being
fiesta	recipient	deity
happiest	spaniel	reinstate

Words with an *-ie* ending:

die	prairie
nightie	tie

And plurals ending in *-ies*:

(fancy)	fancies	(policy)	policies
(harmony)	harmonies	(vacancy)	vacancies

125

Add to this list the word *species,* which has the same form for both singular and plural.

Remember the rest of the *ie* and *ei* spellings by pronunciation.

If the sound is long *e,* the old rule holds true: "*i* before *e* except after *c.*" But only if the sound is long *e*:

ie

achieve	field	hygiene	relief	thief
belief	fiend	lien	relieve	wield
believe	grief	niece	reprieve	yield
brief	grievance	piece	shield	
chief	grieve		shriek	
			siege	

ei

ceiling	conceive	deceive	receipt
conceit	deceit	perceive	receive

When *ie* comes before *r,* the pronunciation is closer to that of short *i* (as in *spirit*):

bier	fierce
tier	pierce

In such cases, however, the spelling pattern follows the same rule: *i* before *e* except after *c.* These words do not form a true exception, since long *e* is regularly pronounced this way before *r*: *mere, near, queer.*

The word *financier* has a *c* before *ie,* but is not really more of an exception than is *policies* or *fancies.* The suffix *-ier* is the same as that of *cashier, cavalier, gondolier,* and *grenadier.*

There are only four absolute exceptions in which *ei* spells long *e* after another consonant:

seize   (with its derivatives *seized, seizure,* and so on)
sheik
weir
weird

The following are also exceptions if you pronounce them with a long *e* (not everyone does):

caffeine	leisure
codeine	neither
either	obeisance
inveigle	protein

In only the following two words *ie* does not spell long *e*:

friend	sieve

REMEMBER: *ie* rather than *ei* spells most of the words with a long *e* sound.

Use *ei* for all other pronunciations, stressed or unstressed:

their	height	counterfeit
heir	kaleidoscope	foreign
heiress	stein	forfeit
	sleight (of hand)	reveille
	seismograph	surfeit

This category also includes a sizable group of words in which *ei* spells long *a*. If the sound is long *a,* use *ei* with no exceptions:

beige	heinous	skein
deign	inveigh	sleigh
eight	neigh	veil
feign	neighbor	vein
feint	reign	weigh
freight	rein	weight

The words **handkerchief** and **mischief** do not have *ei* although the digraphs are unstressed; but you recognize the word **chief** in the last syllable.

SUMMARY: The digraph *ie* is common in word-endings, and in endings it is always easily recognizable (as in **policies, tie,** and **financier**). Otherwise it is used only for the long *e* sound (as in **chief**).

The digraph *ei* is used for the long *e* sound only after *c* (as in **receive**).

ei is used for all other pronunciations.

The EXCEPTIONS: friend   seize
                   sieve   weir
                               weird
                               sheik

The only other exceptions are the eight words that are generally, but not always, pronounced with a long *e* (*either, neither, leisure,* and so on), and also *mischief* and *handkerchief,* which contain the word *chief.*

> Now answer the following questions:
> What is the usual spelling for the long *e* sound?
> What is the usual spelling for all other sounds?
> After what letter does *ei* spell long *e*?
> What are the five absolute exceptions to the *ie-ei* rules?

66· THE DIGRAPH ea

Normally, *ea* spells long *e*, as in *beat, leaf, speak, repeat,* and *yeast.*

But *ea* spells short *e* in the following words:

head	breath	meadow	peasant
bread	leather	dealt	pheasant
instead	weather	endeavor	breakfast
dead	feather	pleasure	ready
tread	health	treasure	heavy
spread	wealth	measure	leaven
dread	stealth	pleasant	heaven
thread	threat	meant	weapon

The past tense of **read** is also pronounced with a short *e* ("red"), even though it is spelled the same as the present tense.

The noun **lead** (metal) belongs in this group also. But the past tense of the verb **lead** ("leed") is spelled **led:**

He contracted *lead* poisoning.
He *led* the horse into the stable.

The digraph *ea* also spells long *a* in a few words:

great steak break

Before *r* plus another consonant *ea* is pronounced "ər":

earl	earth	pearl
early	heard	search
earn	hearse	yearn
earnest	learn	

In one word *ea* is pronounced "ar":

heart

67· THE DIGRAPH ou

Normally, *ou* is used to spell the vowel sound of words like *found, round, devout,* or *aloud.* You also learned a second common use of it in the unstressed ending *-ous: famous, delicious, courteous, tortuous.* It spells a greater variety of vowel sounds than any other digraph, but most of the variations appear in only a few words. It is best to learn these variations individually.

SHORT *u*		SHORT *oo*	*aw*	
country	southern	could	bought	ought
couple	touch	should	brought	sought
cousin	tough	would	cough	trough
double	trouble		fought	wrought
enough	young			
rough				

Before *r, ou* sounds like the *e* in "er" or the *o* in "or":

"er"		"or"	
courage	journey	course	mourn
courtesy	nourish	court	pour
flourish	scourge	four	resources
journal	sojourn	gourd	source

In words of French origin, *ou* often sounds like long *oo*:

boudoir	group
croup	roulette
detour	soup
gourmet	tour

Through, wound, youth, you, and *uncouth* are not French, but share the long *oo* sound.

In several words, *ou* spells long *o*:

boulder	poultry
cantaloupe	shoulder
poultice	soul

68· THE DIGRAPH eu

The digraph *eu* always spells long *u* or long *oo*:

LONG *u*		LONG *oo*	
euphemism	feud	deuce	neutral
Eugene	feudal	leukemia	neutrality
eugenics	therapeutic	maneuver	pneumonia
euphonic		neurotic	rheumatic
		neuter	sleuth

eu is the least common of the long *u* or the long *oo* spellings and appears in only a few words in ordinary usage. Many of this group are technical words.

69· THE DIGRAPHS oo AND oa

Normally, the digraph *oo* spells regular long and short sounds:

LONG *oo: shampoo, fool*
SHORT *oo: stood, wool*

oo is irregular in only four common words:

SHORT *u*	LONG *o*
blood	door
flood	floor

oa is one of the regular digraphs for long *o*: *toast, gloat, load,* and so on. Before *r,* it is pronounced like the *o* in *or:*

boar	hoarse
coarse	oar

In only one word does *oa* spell the sound "aw":

broad

These minor irregularities lead to the frequent confusion between *coarse* and *course.* The Latin root of *course* means "to run," and has given us another modern word, *current.* Most meanings of *course* imply the movement along a path from point to point, whether it is the course of a river or a course of study, a golf course, a course in a meal, or the expression "of course" ("according to ordinary procedure"). Associate the *u* of *run* and *current* with the *u* in *course.*

Coarse, on the other hand, means "crude, unrefined, vulgar, rough."

70· LONG VOWELS BEFORE TWO CONSONANTS

Normally, two consonants together cause the preceding vowel to be short:

lint   past   follow   hanger

A fairly large group of common words has a long vowel before two consonants where you would expect a short one. The long vowels occur mostly before *n, s,* and *l:*

BEFORE *n*		BEFORE *s*	BEFORE *l*	
behind	ancient	bass (voice)	boll	bolt
bind	angel	engross	droll	colt
blind	arrange	gross	knoll	jolt
find	change		poll	revolt

BEFORE *n*		BEFORE *s*	BEFORE *l*	
grind	danger	baste	roll	volt
kind	grange	chaste	stroll	
mind	mange	haste	toll	bolster
ninth	manger	paste	troll	folk
pint	range	pastry		holster
rind	strange	taste	bold	molten
wind	stranger	waste	cold	polka
			fold	soldier
	don't	ghost	hold	upholster
	only	host	mold	yolk
	won't	most	old	
		post	scold	child
			sold	mild
			told	wild

And in a few instances before other letters:

both	chamber	climb	ruthless
catacomb	Christ	comb	truth

ign is always long at the end of words:

align	assign	benign	sign

igh and *ight* are always long:

sigh	high	light	bright

Read aloud the pairs of words below. The one on the left in each pair is spelled regularly, while the one on the right has an irregular long vowel before two consonants:

lint — pint	anger — danger	wind — wind
doll — roll	bewilder — milder	lost — most
boss — gross	flange — range	cloth — both

Note the short vowels in these words ending in *-nge*:

binge	impinge	plunge
hinge	lunge	singe

71· USING o TO SPELL SHORT u

Another group of around seventy words spells the short **u** sound with an **o**, mostly before **n, m,** and **v.** It is believed that many of these words were originally spelled with a **u,** but in the Middle Ages (before the invention of the printing press), scribes used an **o** so as not to confuse the letter **u** with **n, m,** or **v,** which looked very much like it.

once	money	among	stomach	govern
one	honey	come	above	hover
son	month	comfort	covenant	love
sponge	none	company	cover	oven
ton	onion	monk	covet	shove
won	done	monkey	dove	shovel
wonder	front	some	glove	slovenly

Others:

brother	dozen	mother	other
color	from	nothing	smother

An important tip: All these words follow the regular spelling rules for adding suffixes, even though a word that is spelled like a long-vowel word has short-vowel pronunciation. When a suffix beginning with a vowel is added to a word ending in silent **e,** drop the **e** and replace it with the vowel of the suffix:

come	coming	shove	shoving
love	loving	sponge	sponging

The final **e** is retained before a suffix beginning with a consonant:

love	lovely	some	somewhat

A common spelling error is to double the **m** of **_coming_**:

WRONG: comming

Another common error is to spell the short **u** sound in **_among_** like the short **u** in **_young,_** simply because they sound alike:

RIGHT: among   young
WRONG: amoung

This irregular spelling of short **u** also gives several pairs of words that are spelled alike in portions that are pronounced differently:

home — come	bother — brother
bone — none	woven — oven
honk — monk	song — among
frozen — dozen	

72· SILENT CONSONANTS: wr, gn, kn

The unpronounced **w**, **g**, and **k** in **wr**, **gn**, and **kn** stand for sounds which were once spoken, centuries ago, but which have since dropped away. The silent letters remain in the spelling.

Only eighteen words in common usage still begin with **wr**:

wraith	wren	wrinkle
wrangle	wrench	wrist
wrap	wrestle	write
wrath	wretch	writhe
wreath	wriggle	wrong
wreck	wring	wry

Careless errors are sometimes made in mistaking one word for another. Don't let your eye fool you. Slowly read the following pairs of words aloud:

warp	wrap	wrench	wench
wrath	wraith	wring	wiring

Notice that **wrestle** is spelled with an **e**, not an **a**. It is pronounced "resəl" not "rasəl."

Only six words in common usage begin with **gn**, with the **g** silent:

gnarled	gnaw
gnash	gnome
gnat	gnu

Only a few have **gn** at the end. The vowel preceding it is long:

sign	align	deign
assign	malign	feign
consign	benign	reign
design	impugn	
resign		

The word **foreign** is not stressed on the final syllable. Therefore, the vowel sound of **-eign** is neutral rather than long as it would be if stressed.

Again, watch out for reversals in reading or spelling words with **gn** and **ng**:

malign	malinger
signal	single

73· wh: SILENT h OR SILENT w

This combination of letters was once **hw** in English, but somewhere along the way was transposed to **wh.** We still pronounce the **h** before the **w** anyway, as you can tell by putting the palm of your hand in front of your mouth and feeling your breath as you pronounce **whee**! Actually, you say "hwee."

The **h** is now often dropped from the pronunciation of many people, leaving only the **w** sound. Test your pronunciation by holding up your palm an inch from your mouth as you pronounce the following words:

whale	whether	whisper
when	which	white
where	whip	why

Do you pronounce them as if they were spelled like this?

"wale"	"wether"	"wisper"
"wen"	"wich"	"wite"
"ware"	"wip"	"wy"

If so, then you may be making the mistake of sometimes leaving out the *h* also in spelling. Some people who do not pronounce the *h* confuse **whether** with **weather**, **where** with **were**, **which** with **witch**. You do not have to pronounce the *h* to be correct, but be sure you know where to put it in spelling.

In six words beginning with **wh**, the reverse has occurred: *w* is silent and only *h* is pronounced:

who	whole
whom	whore
whose	whooping cough

74· OTHER SILENT w'S

The *w* is silent also in the following four common words:

answer	two
sword	toward

Contrast with **swear**, **sworn**, **twin**, and **coward**.

75· mb

A few words end in the combination **mb**, whose *b* is silent:

bomb	lamb	plumb
crumb	limb	plumber
dumb	numb	succumb
jamb	thumb	

All the words above have short vowels. In a few **mb** words, long vowels have developed irregularly, as you learned in Section 70: **climb**, **comb**, and **catacomb**. Even more irregular than these words are **tomb** and **womb**, where *o* spells long *u*.

76· SILENT L

The three auxiliary verbs, **could**, **would**, and **should**, are written with an *l*, which is not pronounced. It was once pronounced in all three of them, but probably because of weak stress the pronunciation was simplified and the *l* was lost.

Otherwise, *l* is silent only after *a* and *o* in certain words:

calf	calves	walk	chalk
half	halves	talk	stalk
salmon		calm	folk
salve		palm	yolk
		psalm	solder (pronounced
		qualm	"sodder")

Some persons striving for correct pronunciation will try to sound the *l* in these words. But in popular spoken English, it is normally silent. Notice the preservation of *l*, however, in **valve, Ralph,** and **salvation,** and in other words where *l* forms the end of a separate syllable:

calculate   palmetto   salmagundi

After *e, i,* and *u, l* is pronounced normally:

elfin	milk	bulk
elk	silk	hulk

77· mn

Six common words end in the combination **mn,** whose **n** is silent:

autumn	damn
column	hymn
condemn	solemn

Don't forget the *n* when suffixes are added:

condemned	damned
condemning	damning

Each of these words has a related form in which the *n* is pronounced:

autum·nal	dam·nation
colum·nist	hym·nal
condem·nation	solem·nity

A word sometimes mistakenly spelled with **mn** is **dilemma.** It has a double **m** rather than **mn.**

Only one word begins with **mn:**

mnemonic

In this rare instance, the **m** is silent and only the **n** is pronounced. The word means "relating to memory," and is derived from the name of the ancient Greek goddess of memory, Mnemosyne.

78· OTHER SILENT CONSONANTS

Several silent consonants were brought into English spelling in a mistaken attempt to make words look more like their Latin ancestors. Thus we have silent **b** in **debt, doubt,** and **subtle.** These words ought to be spelled *"det," "dout,"* and *"suttle,"* according to our regular system. The Latin ancestors were **debitum, dubitare,** and **subtilis,** from which we also have the words **debit** and **dubious.** In these two words, the **b** is logical and is pronounced. Scholars, in a pedantic zeal to show the relationship of **debt, doubt,** and **subtle** to Latin, added the silent **b,** and it has stayed. The **b** in these three words was never pronounced and could be dropped again with no harm.

In the same fashion, **p** crept into **receipt.** It should be spelled like **deceit** and **conceit.** But it was derived from the Latin **receptus,** "received," and the **p** was inserted in order to show its origin. We are fortunate not to have *"conceipt"* and *"deceipt"* also.

Likewise, the **s** was added to **island** because of the Latin word **insula.** The same unnecessary silent **s** continues in **isle** and **aisle.** There is no excuse for **aisle,** which is not related to **isle** at all, but was mistakenly identified with it through similarity in pronunciation.

Finally, we have two silent *c*'s which were also added to show Latin derivation:

indict   (pronounced "indite")
victuals   (pronounced "vittles")

Indict is modeled after the Latin root *dict-*, and *victuals* is an absurd respelling of a word formerly spelled *"vittles,"* but derived originally from the Latin *victualis*.

A few other words with silent consonants are not recognized as modern respellings. *Psalm* comes from the Latin *psalma*, but had been spelled *"saume"* in English until someone felt it should be restored to its ancient spelling. *Rhyme* was once *"rime,"* but was respelled with *rhy* because of the word *rhythm* from Greek. In this case, there was no Greek word relating to *rhyme* to justify the change. And *rhubarb*, once spelled *"rubarbe,"* was given an *h* in a misguided attempt to show Greek derivation.

These modern respellings all took place at a time when hundreds of scholarly words were being borrowed from Greek and Latin for technical terms in philosophy, science, and medicine. Such new words were not made to conform with native English spelling, but were carried over with many features from their original languages, such as the *rh, pn,* and *ps* combinations of Greek. Needless to say, English-speaking people could not pronounce these combinations and quickly dropped one of the consonants, leaving a silent letter. But it was unfortunate that scholars tried to reform the spelling of other words like *"det," "iland,"* and *"rubarbe,"* which had for centuries been spelled regularly according to the English spelling system.

In the next sections, you will be given other examples of borrowed words which retain their foreign spelling even though many of them have lost their foreign pronunciation.

79· rh

The combination *rh* appears only in words of recent Greek derivation:

rhapsody	diarrhea
rhetoric	catarrh
rheumatism	cirrhosis
rhinoceros	hemorrhage
rhythm	hemorrhoids
	myrrh

These words are always difficult to spell, not only because of the **rh,** but because of doubled **r**'s, **y, eu,** and other odd spellings of unstressed vowels. Only an exceptionally good speller manages to spell all of these words without having to look in a dictionary.

A simple hint will help you remember the medical terms. The combination **rrh** appears in each one of them and no other letter is doubled. The root **hemo-** means "blood" and is familiar in **hemoglobin.** The **m** is never doubled.

80· USING ch TO SPELL "K"

The use of **ch** for the "k" sound is another attempt to spell a Greek letter in English. It appears in a number of very common words:

anchor	Christ	chronic	schedule
bronchitis	Christmas	echo	scheme
character	chorus	mechanic	school
chemical	chrome	orchestra	stomach

The following words are sometimes misspelled or mispronounced:

chaos (pronounced "kay-oss")
chasm
chlorine
melancholy (note the *a* and the single *l* before *y*)
psychic (pronounced "sy-kik"; don't confuse with *physic,* "fiz-ik")

The syllable **arch-** is bothersome in spelling because in some words it is pronounced "ark" and in others "arch" (as in *march*).

We have a "soft" pronunciation in the word *arch* itself (a curved structure used in building) and in *archery*. Several other words with a soft *ch* are: ***archbishop, archduke,*** and other words in which ***arch-*** means chief or foremost, as in ***archfiend*** and ***arch-enemy***; but NOT ***archangel,*** which is pronounced "arkangel."

In most other ***arch-*** words, *ch* spells the hard "k" sound:

archaic	archipelago	architecture
archeology	architect	archives

Other words in which *ch* spells the sound "k":

anarchy	monarchy	strychnine
chord	orchid	synchronize
choreography	parochial	technique
chronicle	patriarch	technical
epoch	pulchritude	
lichen	sepulchre	

81· USING ph TO SPELL "F"

Like *ch,* the digraph *ph* is an attempt to spell a letter in the Greek alphabet. It is always pronounced like the letter *f,* and appears in many common words:

phantom	phenomenon (plural: phenomena)
pharmacy	Philip
phase	trophy
phrase	phony (not a Greek word, but spelled like one)

The Greek roots ***phil-*** (loving), ***-graph*** (writing), ***-phobia*** (fear), ***phon-*** (voice), and ***photo-*** (light), yield many common words:

claustrophobia	(fear of closed places)
philanthropy	(love of mankind)
philosophy	(love of knowledge)
phonograph	(voice-writing)
photograph	(light-writing)
telegraph	(writing from a distance)

The word **saxophone** is derived from the name of its inventor, the Belgian instrument maker A. J. Sax.

Other **ph** words:

aphrodisiac	hyphen	seraph	sylph
emphasis	nephew	sphagnum	syphilis
ephemeral	orphan	sphere	
epitaph	pharaoh	sycophant	

The following words commonly cause difficulty in both pronunciation and spelling because of the unusual combination of letters and sounds:

diphtheria	diphthong	naphtha
(dif·ther·i·a)	(dif·thong)	(naf·tha)

Many people, confused by seeing **phth,** drop an **h** and pronounce the **p** alone: "dip·thong," "nap·tha."

Pamphlet confuses a hesitant speller too, perhaps because he reads *"pamp-"* rather than **pamph-,** and sometimes reverses the sounds into *"phamplet."*

One word has **pph:**

sapphire

ph is a consonant digraph, with a single sound, like **th** or **ch.** The two letters sometimes come together, however, without forming a digraph. In such cases they are usually recognizable as two separate sounds:

haphazard   shepherd

82· ps, pn, pt

The **p** is silent in these combinations when they appear at the beginning of words. The roots **pseudo** (false) and **psyche** (soul) yield most of the common words with these letters:

pseudoclassic	psychiatry
pseudonym	psychic
	psychology
	psychopath

The Greek words for lung and breath give us *pneumonia* and *pneumatic.*

Apart from a few technical words, *pt* is found only in *ptomaine* and *ptarmigan.*

83· FRENCH WORDS

Words borrowed from French a long time ago have gradually been absorbed into our spelling system until they no longer offer a problem in either spelling or pronunciation. For example: *beef, pork, perfect, finish, poor.* But many words recently borrowed still retain their French spelling and often their French pronunciation.

Below are lists of such words with a guide to pronunciation. Notice that the stress often falls on the last syllable, whereas in native English words it is generally on the first.

eau Spells Long o ||||||||||||||||||||||||||||||||||||||||||||||||||||||||||

beau	plateau
bureau	trousseau
chateau	

Beauty and *beautiful* have been Anglicized in pronunciation, though French spelling remains. Notice the pronunciation of *eau* in *bureaucracy.* The original long *o* has changed to short *o.*

i Spells Long e ||||||||||||||||||||||||||||||||||||||||||||||||||||||||||

cuisine	marine	sardine
gaberdine	nicotine	tambourine
limousine	quarantine	tangerine
machine	ravine	
magazine	routine	
aperitif	elite	police
automobile	modiste	prestige
caprice	motif	regime
cerise	naive	suite
chemise	petite	valise

qu Spells "k" ‖‖‖‖‖‖‖‖‖‖‖‖‖‖‖‖‖‖‖‖‖‖‖‖‖‖‖‖‖‖‖‖‖‖

antique	grotesque	picturesque
burlesque	liquor	physique
clique	mannequin	piquant
conquer	masquerade	pique
coquette	mystique	plaque
critique	oblique	technique
etiquette	opaque	unique

gue Spells "g," ngue Spells "ng" ‖‖‖‖‖‖‖‖‖‖‖‖‖‖‖‖‖‖‖‖‖‖‖‖‖‖‖‖

colleague	intrigue	plague
fatigue	league	prologue
fugue	meringue	vague
harangue	morgue	vogue

The word **rogue** is of unknown origin, but follows the French spelling pattern. **Tongue** is a native English word and should be spelled *"tung,"* but it has been modeled on French spelling also.

gn Spells "ny" as in canyon ‖‖‖‖‖‖‖‖‖‖‖‖‖‖‖‖‖‖‖‖‖‖‖‖‖‖‖‖‖‖‖‖

chignon	poignant
cognac	vignette

ch Spells "sh" ‖‖‖‖‖‖‖‖‖‖‖‖‖‖‖‖‖‖‖‖‖‖‖‖‖‖‖‖‖‖

brochure	charlatan	chevron	cliché
chagrin	chauffeur	chic	machine
champagne	chef	chiffon	mustache
chaperon	chenille	chivalry	parachute

ge Spells "zh" ‖‖‖‖‖‖‖‖‖‖‖‖‖‖‖‖‖‖‖‖‖‖‖‖‖‖‖‖‖

barrage	corsage	massage	regime
beige	entourage	menage	rouge
camouflage	espionage	mirage	sabotage
collage	fuselage	montage	

The **ge** of **garage** is generally Anglicized to the sound of the **ge** in *age*.

Final **t** is Silent; **et** Spells Long **a** ‖‖‖‖‖‖‖‖‖‖‖‖‖‖‖‖‖‖‖‖‖‖‖‖‖‖‖‖‖‖‖‖‖‖‖‖‖‖

ballet	cabaret	croquet	ricochet
beret	chalet	gourmet	sachet
bouquet	Chevrolet	parfait	valet
buffet	crochet	parquet	'
depot	esprit	debut	ragout

Final **e** or **ee** Spells Long **a** ‖‖‖‖‖‖‖‖‖‖‖‖‖‖‖‖‖‖‖‖‖‖‖‖‖‖‖‖‖‖‖‖‖‖‖‖‖‖

café	fiancé (masculine)		risqué
cliché	fiancée (feminine)		sauté
communiqué	matinee	passé	soiree
divorcée	melee	pâté	soufflé
entrée	naiveté	résumé	toupee

The accent mark is always used on certain of these words, as shown above. In several cases, the accent mark serves to distinguish the vowel from a silent *e* in similar English words like *resume* and *pate.*

The ending *-ee* has been Anglicized in many words, such as *devotee, employee,* and *absentee,* and is pronounced like long *e.*

en and **in** ‖‖

Since speakers in English usually cannot pronounce the French nasalized *en* and *in,* these sounds are simplified to "on" and "an" respectively:

encore	entrée	ingenue
en masse	entrepreneur	meringue
ennui	genre	
	rendezvous	

oi Spells "wa" as in **water** ‖‖‖

au revoir	coiffure	soiree
boudoir	reservoir	repertoire (Anglicized form: repertory)

eu ||||||||||||||||||||||||||||||||||||||||||||||||||||||||||||

amateur	chauffeur	liqueur
chanteuse	fleur de lys	milieu
chartreuse	grandeur	poseur

Probably few people except those who have studied French attempt to pronounce these words accurately with the neutral vowel sound they have in French. Instead, the endings of these words are becoming Anglicized to correspond with the sounds of the English endings *-ure, -er,* or *-use.* The *eu* in *maneuver* has become long *u,* and the *ieu* in *lieu* and *lieutenant* has become long *oo.*

ou Spells Long **oo** ||||||||||||||||||||||||||||||||||||||||||||||||||||||||||||||

boudoir	gourmet	silhouette
bouquet	louver	tour de force
crouton	mousse	
detour	roulette	

In *boulevard* and *bourgeois,* *ou* has already shifted from long *oo* to short *oo,* as in *wool* and *poor.* The first syllable of *journal* has been shortened even further, to "jernǝl." Also, many people say "bo-kay" rather than "boo-kay" for *bouquet.*

Odds and Ends ||||||||||||||||||||||||||||||||||||||||||||||||||||||||||||

chaise longue: This interesting two-part word is rapidly becoming absorbed into our pronunciation system. The French pronunciation approaches "shez long" (the *ng* is nasalized and cannot be accurately represented here). Americans generally pronounce it "chase lounge," mistaking the word *longue* for *lounge.* Literally translated, it means "long chair," not "lounge chair."

chamois: "shammy"

chassis: "shassy" or "chassy"

cologne: *gn* has been simplified to "n," as in *bone.*

corps: silent *ps,* "core"

coup: silent *p,* "coo"

debris: silent *s,* "dǝBREE"

facade: *c* spells "s"; *-ade* has *a* as in *father*.

liaison: three syllables: *li·ai·son*, "LEEəzon"

locale, *morale*, *musicale*: stress on the last syllable, which has a short *a* and rhymes with *pal*

papier mâché: Pronounce "papər məSHAY"; note *-ier* in *papier*.

personnel: This is probably the most often misspelled French word in English. It is stressed on the last syllable: "person-NEL." It is confused with the regular English word *personal*, which has no doubled consonants. Remember that words of more than one syllable normally do not double a final *l* unless formed from a root word which ends in a doubled *l*: *enroll*, *fulfill*.

porpoise, *tortoise*: Unstressed ending gives "porpəs," "tortəs."

questionnaire: Notice the double *n*.

renaissance: Remember it as *re·naissance*, which means literally "re·birth." Thus there is no reason to double the *n*. When used as the name of a period in history, it is capitalized.

suede: "swade"

84· SILENT h

In addition to its place in the combination *rh*, the letter *h* is occasionally silent elsewhere. It seldom causes spelling difficulty in the few words that begin with silent *h*:

heir	honest	hour	honor

or in the following words, which have a silent *h* in some people's pronunciation:

herb	humor	human	humble

It is likely to be left out, however, where it comes in the middle of a word:

annihilate	exhilarate	gingham	silhouette
exhaust	exhort	prohibition	upholster
exhibit	exhume	shepherd	vehement

Learn these words by syllables: *ex·haust, up·hol·ster, an·ni·hil·ate.* They are mostly regular except for the silent *h.*

85· gh

Although only a few dozen words have the irregular combination *gh,* they have long been famous as examples of how illogical English spelling can be. In reality, only a few of them cause any serious spelling difficulty.

gh appears at the beginning of only five common words:

> ghastly   ghost
> gherkin   ghoul
> ghetto

The *h* in *gherkin* and *ghetto* is considered necessary to keep the hard sound of *g,* as it keeps the *g* hard in *spaghetti;* otherwise the words would be pronounced "jerkin" and "jetto." The letter *h* plays the same role in *dinghy,* which otherwise would look identical to *dingy* with its soft *g. Ghoul* is from Arabic; the Arabic *h* represents a strong breathy sound we do not have in English.

Sorghum is modern scientific Latin and should never have been given an *h,* for it is unnecessary in either meaning or pronunciation.

At the end of words, *gh* has only one consonant sound, that of *f:*

> laugh   enough   cough
> laughter   rough   trough
>   slough
>   tough

The word *slough,* when used as a verb meaning "to cast off," is pronounced "sluff" to rhyme with *rough* and *tough.* The same spelling is also pronounced with an open vowel sound and silent *gh,* to rhyme with either *through* or *bough.* Then it means either "a place of deep mud or mire," or "a bog."

Usually, **gh** is silent and follows either a long vowel or the special vowel sounds **au** and **ou**.

ight and igh ||||||||||||||||||||||||||||||||||||||||||||||||||||||||||||||

blight	fright	right	high
bright	light	sight	sigh
delight	might	slight	nigh
fight	night	tight	thigh
flight	plight		

The word **wright** is often misunderstood. It means a skilled worker or creator, and is related to **wrought**, an archaic verb form of **work** used now only in a few expressions like "wrought iron," "well-wrought," and "wrought up." **Wright** appears in a few compound words like **wheelwright, shipwright,** and **play-wright.** A **playwright** is a professional maker of plays. Don't confuse **wright** with **write;** there is no such word as *"playwrite."*

eigh ||||||||||||||||||||||||||||||||||||||||||||||||||||||||||||||

Words containing **eigh** were reviewed in Section 65 at the beginning of this chapter. Examples:

eight	neighbor
freight	weigh

With the exception of **height** and **sleight** (of hand), they all have a long **a** sound. Without exception, they are spelled with **ei** rather than **ie.**

The word **straight** is the only one which has the digraph **ai.**

aught and ought ||||||||||||||||||||||||||||||||||||||||||||||||||||||||||||||

aught	haughty	bought	ought
caught	naughty	brought	sought
daughter	onslaught	fought	thought
distraught	slaughter	nought	wrought
fraught	taught		

Up to this point, the **gh** words fall into regular patterns and need not cause any problem in spelling. The less familiar words ending in **-aught** and **-ought** may occasionally be confused; but otherwise, **gh** simply is part of a regular long-vowel spelling in a few small groups of words.

The troublemakers are the approximately half-dozen words which end in an open vowel sound spelled **-ough:**

LONG *o*	LONG *oo*	*ou* (AS IN *out*)
although	through	bough
dough		
furlough		
thorough		
though		

Of these words, three are often confused by the hesitant speller:

though	through	thorough

Confusion occurs because the eye does not see the **r** soon enough, or does not put it in the right sequence:

tho-	thro-	thor-

These words are very often spelled **tho, thru,** and **thoro** in popular usage that may someday be accepted as formally correct. **Through** already appears as **thru** on highway signs: **thruway.** This improvement would be desirable.

To confuse the two words **huge** and **Hugh** is to reveal a failure in understanding the simplest regularities in our spelling system. Yet the spelling "*hugh*" for **huge** appears surprisingly often in student writing. In the first place, **huge** is completely regular: long **u** is followed by **-ge** which indicates a soft **g** sound. **Hugh** has the irregular combination **gh,** which is usually silent and is preceded by a long vowel. This word, too, is regular for that small group of words ending in **gh.** In a few words **gh** has the consonant sound of **f;** but under no circumstances could it possibly indicate the sound of **-ge.**

86· sc

According to our basic rule, **c** is pronounced "k" before **a, o,** or **u:**

scarf	discount	discursive
cascade	misconduct	miscue
escape	scowl	sculpture

The combination *sc* is pronounced "s" only before *e* and *i*. It is easiest to remember when it comes at the beginning of a word:

scene	science	scion
scent	scimitar	scissors
scepter	scintillate	scythe

When *sc* comes in the middle or near the end of a word, it is harder to recognize:

abscess	discipline	acquiescent	acquiesce
adolescence	fascinate	convalescence	convalesce
ascend	irascible	effervescent	effervesce
ascertain	lascivious	fluorescent	fluoresce
condescend	miscellaneous	reminiscent	reminisce
crescent	muscle	incandescent	
descend	oscillate	iridescent	
descent	resuscitate	obsolescence	
discern	transcend		
disciple	viscera		

However, it is usually easier to remember the *-sce* ending than the *uo* in *fluoresce* or the *acq* in *acquiesce.*

The difficulty really arises, as always, among a few pairs of words that look and sound somewhat alike. The *sc* is more likely to creep in where it doesn't belong than it is likely to be left out. The Latin root word determines whether *sc* is in the spelling. For example, the Latin verb *scandere* (to climb) is the source of *ascend*, *descend* (and *descent*), *transcend,* and *condescend.* But the following words do not have the same root and therefore no *c:*

absence	essence	presence
decent	license	recent

The hesitant speller may have little trouble with these words but come to a standstill over the problem of *sc* when it is pronounced "sh." The worry is largely unnecessary, since *sc* is an extremely uncommon spelling for this sound. As usual, no more than a half-dozen words cause all the difficulty.

First, refresh your memory with the fact that virtually all the words ending in *-cious, -cial,* or *-cian* are spelled with *c* alone:

gracious	commercial	mathematician
precious	special	technician

The only EXCEPTIONS are *luscious* and *conscious.*

The Latin verb *scire* (to know) is the source of all the other words in which *sci* spells "sh." Examples:

conscience	omniscience
conscientious	omniscient

In each of these words you can recognize the similarity to the related word *science.*

Crescendo is the only word in which *sc* spells "sh" before an *e.* Its pronunciation is modern Italian, from which it was borrowed.

87· LL

British practice is irregular and somewhat inconsistent in doubling the final *l* when a suffix is added. Because we often read articles and books printed in England, we may develop unnecessary confusion over this spelling. American practice follows the regular pattern which you have already learned.

If a word of more than one syllable ends in *l,* the *l* is doubled before a vowel only if stress falls on the last syllable:

DOUBLING		NO DOUBLING	
annul	annulled	total	totaled
control	controlling	tranquil	tranquilizer
metal	metallic	travel	traveling
tranquil	tranquillity		

If the suffix begins with a consonant, the *l* is not doubled:

annul   annulment

One-syllable words normally end in doubled *l*:

roll   fill

This doubled *l* is retained when prefixes are added:

enroll   fulfill

You will remember that *ful* is always spelled with a single *l* when used as a prefix or suffix. It is spelled *full* only when used as a separate word. The further addition of suffixes give us **enrollment** and **fulfillment.**

When **-ly** is added to words that already end in *ll,* one of the *l*'s is dropped:

dull	dully
full	fully
skill	skilless

Otherwise, we would have three *l*'s in a row: *"fullly."*

Only a few irregularities remain. When a suffix is added to **symbol, alcohol,** and **idol,** the final *l* is not doubled in spite of stress on the last syllable:

symbolic   alcoholic   idolatry

The word **whole** drops the **e** before **-ly:**

wholly

Cancel and **crystal** would normally not double the *l* before a suffix beginning with a vowel because they are not stressed on the last syllable. **Canceled** and **canceling** are regular, but the irregular **cancellation** is the preferred spelling. **Crystal** doubles the *l* before all suffixes beginning with a vowel:

crystallize   crystalline   crystalloid

The problem of a doubled *l* is bothersome only in a few longer words where *ll* occurs somewhere in the middle:

artillery	parallel	scintillate
constellation	penicillin	syllable
malleable	satellite	tonsillitis

One small group of words is perfectly regular but causes more misspellings than all the others. These words begin with **al-**:

almighty	although
almost	altogether
already	always
also	

The difficulty is caused by confusing the prefix **al-** with the separate word **all**. Notice the difference in meaning:

> The papers are *all* together in one pile.
> Henry is *altogether* too ambitious.

Altogether means "completely" or "entirely."
    Already and **all ready** also have different meanings:

> It is *already* too late.
> The packages are *all ready* to go.

At present, the spelling *"alright"* is not considered acceptable. Perhaps someday it will be. But until then, the expression must be spelled as two separate words: **all right**.

Otherwise, when **all** enters into a compound with other words it is hyphenated:

all-powerful	all-round
all-purpose	all-star

The one EXCEPTION: **allspice**.

The general rule, then, is that **all** has only one *l* in compounds, just like **ful**. Otherwise it is a separate word.

NOTE: Your dictionary may tell you that the British system of doubling final *l* after unstressed syllables is also acceptable in this country. For example: **traveller, revelling**. But it is easier to keep to the regular principle governing such endings and not make an exception for *l*.

88· u IN PECULIAR PLACES

You have seen (Section 83) how *u* appears in the French word-ending *-gue*, creating a hard *g*. As you know, *-ge* (without the *u*) is always soft. The word *vague,* for example, would rhyme with *rage* if it were not for the insertion of *u* after the *g*.

In a few other words, a silent *u* also follows a hard *g* or *c,* and serves to indicate a hard rather than a soft sound:

disguise	guest	guilt	biscuit
guess	guide	guitar	circuit
guerrilla	guild	guy	

The word *guard* (with its derivatives *guardian, guardian-ship,* and so on) has inherited a silent *u* for no good reason, since the *g* is normally hard before *a* anyway. *Guarantee* is the only other word with this irregular spelling. Don't let two such exceptions interfere with your regular spelling of words such as *regard* or *garnish,* which have syllables with the same sound.

u has the sound of *w* in a few words:

anguish	language	persuade
distinguish	languish	qualm
guava	penguin	squad

u is silent in *languor,* just as it is in *liquor* and other words of French origin.

Buoy is pronounced "boo-ee" by many people, who will have no trouble remembering the *u.* But if you pronounce it "boy," you must remember the silent *u,* which appears also in the related word *buoyancy.*

u also has no logical place in *build, building,* and *buy,* in which the *u* is not pronounced.

89· acq AND aq

The troublesome combination *acq* is another minor variation which occurs in only a few words, but is apt to creep by mistake into places where it does not belong. Only the four following common words, with their related forms, begin with **acq-**:

> acquaint (acquaintance, acquainted, . . .)
> acquiesce (acquiescence, . . .)
> acquire (acquired, acquisition, . . .)
> acquit (acquitted, acquittal, . . .)

Words derived from the Latin **aqua** (water) account for most words that begin simply with **aq-**:

> aquarium   aqueduct
> aquatic   aqueous

Notice that French words such as **croquet, plaque,** or **opaque** do not have a **c** before the **q**.

PART IV

Downright Irregularities and Further Ways to Avoid Misspelling

We come at last to the relatively few remaining words whose spelling does not match pronunciation according to any of the regular patterns. Many such words—like *friend, sieve, blood,* and *straight*—have already been given to you as exceptions. These words are only one or two of a kind and should not be cited as evidence of how irregular our spelling system is generally. It does happen, however, that a few dozen irregular words are in such common usage that they seem to be far more numerous than they really are.

90· IRREGULAR WORDS IN DAILY USE

Short vowels where you would expect long ones:

have	again
give	against
gone	been
live	does
were	said
	says

The verbs *have, give,* and *live,* in spite of their pronunciation, behave in spelling just like long-vowel words. The *e* is dropped before a suffix beginning with a vowel:

> have   having
> give   giver
> live   lived

Said is an irregular past-tense spelling like *laid* and *paid.* Normally, when a root word ends in *-ay,* *-ed* is added without any change: *pray—prayed, dismay—dismayed, relay—relayed.* But the three verbs *say,* *lay,* and *pay* change *y* to *i* and add only *-d.*

Other vowels which behave differently from what is expected:

do	prove	any	what	sew
into	to	many	was	
lose	two			
move	who			

Words of such frequent occurrence are all, luckily, quite short. They must simply be memorized individually until they can be spelled correctly without conscious effort.

91· ONE OR TWO OF A KIND

The following words all contain unusual spellings, mostly of vowels. These are the real rarities, some of which have a spelling found only in a single word:

ache: A native Old English word which ought to be spelled *"ake,"* but which was remodeled on the Greek *ch* by mistake. An old-fashioned spelling puzzle was to ask someone to pronounce a word broken down into these supposed syllables: *"bac·kac·he."* Virtually no one recognized it as *backache.*

bosom: *o* spells short *oo.*

bury: With its derivative *burial,* this is the only word in which *u* spells short *e.*

busy: With its derivative *business,* this is the only word in which *u* spells short *i.*

canoe: Not likely to be misspelled, but the only word besides *shoe* which uses *oe* to spell long *oo.*

choir: One of the most illogical spellings in the English language. It came to us through French from the Greek word *chorus.*

colonel: Pronounced "kernəl." An old spelling *"coronel"* survives in the pronunciation.

fiery: Not the expected form, *"fire + y,"* but *fi·er·y.*

fuchsia: The only word in which *chs* spells "sh." The flower is named after a German botanist, Leonard Fuchs.

gauge: The only word in which *au* spells long *a*: "gage."

hiccough: It is better to spell this word *hiccup,* since this spelling is also acceptable. *-cough* never represented the actual pronunciation, but replaced *cup* simply by analogy with the word *cough.* No one actually says "hik-koff."

isthmus and *asthma*: Two words with silent *th.* The word *clothes* is also usually pronounced as if spelled *"close"* (silent *th*).

leopard, jeopardy, jeopardize, Leonard, Geoffrey: *eo* spells short *e.*

margarine: The only word in which *g* is soft before *a.*

people: The only word in which *eo* spells long *e.*

plaid: The digraph *ai* spells short *a.*

quay: Pronounced like the word *key.* Both *quay* and *key* have irregular digraphs for long *e.*

sergeant: The first syllable is pronounced "sar," in the British fashion. Americans say *clerk* and *Berkeley* with an "er," rather than as the British: "clark" and "Barkley."

woman and *women*: The difference between singular and plural is indicated in the spelling of the final syllables *-man* and *-men.* But in speaking, the difference is indicated by vowel change in the first syllable: "woomən" (short *oo*) and "wimən." *Women* is the only word in which *o* spells short *i.*

yacht: A Dutch word, whose *ch* has become silent because it does not correspond with any English sound. Yet the *a* retains its continental pronunciation.

92· WORDS COMMONLY MISSPELLED THROUGH ADDING OR OMITTING LETTERS

Words of more than one syllable often lack, in speaking, some of the sounds shown in spelling. You already know how unstressed vowels are slurred over. Not only vowels but also consonants and whole syllables sometimes disappear in pronunciation. For example, no one pronounces the *t* in **Christmas** or the first *d* in **Wednesday** ("Wensdy"). This silence is not a fault in the speaker, since it is natural and unavoidable that unstressed sounds should lose identity or be lost altogether. Don't try to make your speech conform with spelling, since this is virtually impossible. Just learn the accepted spellings as they now exist, and hope that someday spelling will conform more closely with speaking. In the meantime, it will help you to remember certain words if you realize which letters are often mistakenly omitted in spelling because they are often not pronounced.

CORRECT SPELLING	COMMON ERROR
actually	various letters omitted or misplaced, because of pronunciation "*ackshəlly*"
attempts	*t* omitted: "*attemps*"
cupboard	*p* omitted (*b* added): "*cubbord*"
deteriorate	*or* omitted: "*deteriate*"
diamond	*a* omitted: "*dimond*"
environment	syllables reversed: "*enviornment*"; sometimes *n* omitted also: "*enviorment*." Remember the word *iron* is in it.
every	*e* omitted: "*evry*"
further	first *r* omitted: "*futher*" (in some dialects the *r* is not distinctly pronounced)
government	*n* omitted: "*goverment*"
mortgage	*t* omitted: "*morgage*"
probably	*ab* omitted: "*probly*"
quantity	*t* omitted: "*quanity*"
raspberry	*p* omitted: "*rasberry*"
recognize	*g* omitted: "*reconize*"
several	*e* omitted: "*sevral*"
sophomore	*o* omitted: "*sophmore*"
succeed	*c* omitted: "*suceed*"
surprise	*r* omitted: "*suprise*"
temperament	*a* omitted: "*temperment*"
temperature	*a* omitted: "*temperture*"

CORRECT SPELLING	COMMON ERROR
vacuum	one *u* omitted (final *e* added) : *"vacume"*
vineyard	*e* omitted (which does not indicate a long vowel) : *"vinyard"*

In the following words, letters are added or transposed:

athlete	*a* or *e* added: *"athalete," "athelete"*
nuclear	letters transposed: *"nucular"*

A similar error is to leave off a plural *s*; for example, plurals of words that end in *-st*:

SINGULAR	PLURAL
dentist	dentist*s*
psychologist	psychologist*s*

The plural *s* after *-st* is seldom clearly spoken, and may be carelessly omitted in writing.

The ending *-er* is also sometimes forgotten when it follows a similar sounding syllable:

manufacture manufactur*er*

The word **used** is heard often in the phrase, "I used to . . ." The **d** of **used** disappears from pronunciation, so that the word may be misspelled in writing as simply *"use": "*I use to." Be sure to keep the verb in past tense, **used.**

Words ending in **ct** often lose the final **t** in pronunciation:

strict abject precinct

This loss occurs especially when a suffix is added:

strictly (NOT *"strickly"*)
abjectly (NOT *"abjeckly"*)

93· CHANGES IN FORM THAT CAUSE MISTAKES

A few words do not follow the regular pattern when suffixes are added, but drop letters that normally would be kept. Here, the reverse kind of error is often made and letters are inserted which should be left out:

DROP THE *e*
WHEN ADDING SUFFIXES

disaster	disastrous
hinder	hindrance
launder	laundry
remember	remembrance
winter	wintry
wonder	wondrous

Lightning is similarly formed from the verb *lighten,* which once meant "to flash." We also have the spelling *lightening,* which means "making less heavy": the *lightening* of a load. *Hungrily* is formed regularly from *hungry* by changing *y* to *i* when *-ly* is added.

For one reason or another, a few words shift in vowel spelling when changed in form:

curious   curiosity

The two endings are *-ous* and *-osity.* Do NOT put a *u* in *-osity.*

When the suffix *-ation* is added to *pronounce,* the *ou* shifts to *u:*

pronounce   pronunciation

The word *gaiety* is simple but often misspelled because of the three vowel letters in a row. The *y* of *gay* shifts to *i,* the suffix *-ety* is added: *gai·ety.* The digraph *ai* spells the long *a* sound.

Forty is not the word *four* with *-ty* added. Be careful not to put a *u* in it.

four   fourteen   forty

Ninety is regular in adding *-ty* to *nine.* But *ninth* is irregular in dropping the *e* before *-th:*

nine   ninety   ninth

94· WORDS EASILY MISTAKEN FOR EACH OTHER

If you learned to read whole words too rapidly before you learned how they were formed syllable by syllable, you probably have a bad habit of mistaking many words at first glance just because they have a similar over-all appearance. You can correct this habit only by training yourself to group the letters of a word in their proper order, syllable by syllable.

Several exercises have already been given for practice in distinguishing words that look alike. Here is another. Read the following words to yourself; then have someone dictate them as you write them:

tried	sacred	salve	through
tired	scared	slave	thorough
cruelty	interpret	avid	though
cruelly	interrupt	avoid	martial
anecdote	charter	blot	marital
antidote	character	bolt	united
soldier	irreverent	formerly	untied
solider	irrelevant	formally	calvary
form	flatter	bias	cavalry
from	falter	basis	statue
fired	abominable	ingenuous	stature
fried	abdominal	ingenious	nuclear
		closet	unclear
		closest	

Even if you make no mistakes of inaccurate reading, you may be hesitant about the spelling of the following groups of words.

lose, loose, loss ||||||||||||||||||||||||||||||||||||||||||||||||||||||||||||||||||

Lose is irregular, like *move* and *prove*, for the *o* has a long *oo* sound. The usual mistake is to write *loose* when you mean *lose*. The *s* in *loose* is hissed; it rhymes with *goose*. You may have *loose* change in your pocket, but you *lose* money. *Loss* is perfectly regular; it rhymes with *boss*.

their, there, they're ||||||||||||||||||||||||||||||||||||||||||||||||||||||||||||||||||

Their means "belonging to them": *their* country, *their* business, *their* marriage.

There is a direction (opposite of ***here***) : "You'll enjoy living ***there.***" It also is used in the phrases "***there*** is" and "***there*** are": "***There*** are eighteen inhabitants per square mile."

They're is a contraction of ***they are***: "***They're*** the only friends I have."

its, it's ||||||||||||||||||||||||||||||||||||||||||||||||||||||||||||||||||

This problem is really one of punctuation, but since these words are always given in spelling lists, they will be treated here.

It is almost impossible to misspell ***its***. But it also seems almost impossible for many people to learn when to put an apostrophe in it.

It's means "it is." It is a contraction, like ***don't*** (for "do not"), ***won't*** (for "will not"), ***I'll*** (for "I will"), ***John's coming*** (for "John is coming"), ***I'd have*** (for "I would have"), and so forth.

MEMORIZE: ***it's*** means only "it is."

Without an apostrophe, ***its*** is a possessive pronoun. No pronoun takes an apostrophe in any possessive form: ***his, hers, theirs, ours, its.***

There is no such form at "*its'*," where the apostrophe follows the ***s***. There is only ***it's***, which means only one thing: ***it is.***

choose, chose ||||||||||||||||||||||||||||||||||||||||||||||||||||||||||||||||

Both these spellings are regular. Don't be misled by ***lose*** into writing ***chose*** (rhymes with ***rose***) when you mean ***choose***:

> *Choose* the color you like best.
> He *chose* the red one.

moral, morale; local, locale ||||||||||||||||||||||||||||||||||||||||||||||||||||||||||||||||||||||||

When ***e*** is added, the stress shifts to the last syllable, but the vowel is short, rhyming with *pal*. (See Section 83, French Words.) ***Morale*** is a state of mind: "The troops have maintained a high ***morale***." ***Locale*** is a place or locality, usually thought of as the scene or setting of some action or event. It is often used with reference to a work of literature: "The ***locale*** of Lewis's novel is a small Minnesota town."

Moral and ***local*** are stressed on the first syllable, and are adjectives: "***moral*** behavior," "***local*** color."

principle, principal ||||||||||||||||||||||||||||||||||||||||||||||||||||||||||||

Do you recognize the common *-al* ending of one of these? It is like *local, vital, final, classical*—all adjectives. *Principal* means "first in rank or importance": "His *principal* reason for leaving was to get a better job." The head of a school is also a *principal*, because he is "first in rank or importance."

A *principle*, on the other hand, is a general truth or moral standard: "the *principle* of equality"; "the *principle* of honesty"; "a man of high *principles*."

prophecy, prophesy ||||||||||||||||||||||||||||||||||||||||||||||||||||||||||||

The first is a noun: "No one believed the *prophecy* that war would break out in September."

The second is a verb: "Can he *prophesy* the outcome of the election?" *Prophesy* has a secondary stress on the last syllable: "*PROPH·e·SIGH.*" *Prophecy*, like *pharmacy*, has no stress on the last syllable.

alter, altar ||||||||||||||||||||||||||||||||||||||||||||||||||||||||||||

Alter means "to change something." An *altar* is in a church.

affect, effect ||||||||||||||||||||||||||||||||||||||||||||||||||||||||||||

Affect (verb): to act upon, or to influence. "How will foreign affairs *affect* the election?"

Effect (noun): a result or consequence. "The President's assassination had a profound *effect* on all of us."

Learn these two most common uses first. Below are some additional examples:

> Early frost last year in vegetable-growing areas *affected* food prices.
> The accident has *affected* the way he uses his left arm.
> The *effect* of the early frost last year was to raise food prices.
> The scientist studies cause and *effect*.

Only when you clearly understand these two meanings are you ready for a third:

Effect (verb): to bring about, to produce, achieve, or accomplish. Some examples of the use of this verb are:

> The doctor *effected* a complete cure.
> Four prisoners *effected* an escape during the night.

This is the usage you are least likely to employ. The difference between the two verbs is important. You can usually test your choice by substituting the verb *influence* for *affect* and *bring about* for *effect.*

Finally, the word *affect* has one minor use as a noun. It is a technical term used in psychology to denote an emotional stimulus. When so used, the stress is on the first syllable: *AF · fect.* Because of its unique pronunciation, it is not likely to be confused with other uses of the word.

than, then |||||:|||||||||||||||||||||||||||||||||||||||||||||||||||||

Then refers to a time:

> He became a friend of John Steinbeck, who was *then* a
> student at Stanford University.
> She was *then* known by her maiden name.

Then is frequently used to clarify the order of items in a sequence:

> He visited the Philippines, *then* Indonesia, Burma, and
> Ceylon; then India and Pakistan; and finally Afghanistan.

Then may also express a logical connection or consequence:

> If *you* can, *then* so can I.

Than is used only in comparison or contrast:

> Easier said *than* done.
> He'd rather sleep *than* work.
> She is more mature *than* most girls her age.

Than has no reference to time or sequence of events. A common error is to spell *then* when you mean *than.*

> WRONG: Harold is taller then Gene.

desert, dessert ||||||||||||||||||||||||||||||||||||||||||||||||||||||||||||

Dessert (a serving of food, usually sweet, after a meal) is one of only three words in which *ss* is pronounced "z." The others are *possess* and *scissors*. Normally, *ss* has a hissed "s" sound, as in *passive* or *lesson*. *Dessert* is stressed on the last syllable. The doubled *s* somehow makes it look as if it ought to be stressed on the first syllable instead, like *dressing*. For these reasons, *dessert* is a troublesome word. Remember the two *s*'s by thinking "sweet stuff." The similar word *desert*, with only one *s*, is spelled regularly.

moment, memento ||||||||||||||||||||||||||||||||||||||||||||||||||||||||||||||

Memento is related to **memory**, not to *moment*. Put *e* rather than *o* in the first syllable.

to, too ||||||||||||||||||||||||||||||||||||||||||||||||||||||||||

Too means either "also" or "too much":

I, *too*, have suffered.
Ralph is *too* restless.

Too is always stressed in a sentence; *to* is usually unstressed:

I would like *to* go *too*.

95·PREFIXES MISTAKEN FOR EACH OTHER

You learned in Part I (Section 32) how *in-* and *en-* can be confused. Several other prefixes sound somewhat alike and can also be mistaken for each other.

pre-, pro-, per- |||||||||||||||||||||||||||||||||||||||||||||||||||||||||||||||||

pre- means "before," as in *preschool.*
pro- means "forward," or "in favor of," as in *progress* and *pro-American.*
per- means either "through," as in *perforate* and *percolate*; or "completely," as in *perfect* and *pernicious.*

Only **pre-** and **pro-** have easily recognizable meanings, although not in every case. The Latin background is lost on the modern speller, who can't be expected to remember these prefixes according to their Latin meanings. **Pre-** and **pro-** are live prefixes and enter into the formation of new words like **preadolescent** and **prodemocracy.** But few people can readily see the meaning of the prefix in **professor, produce, pronounce, protest,** or **protect.**

Rather than trying to remember English by learning Latin, you will do best simply to classify each word in your mind as either **pre-, pro-,** or **per-** and to try to remember it accordingly, so you won't write *"perfessor"* for **professor,** or *"pretain"* for **pertain.** Below are the most common words whose prefixes might be confused:

pre-	pro-	per-
predicament	profess	perceive
predict	profound	percussion
prefer	profusion	perforate
preliminary	pronounce	perform
prerequisite	propose	persevere
prerogative	provoke	persist
prescription		personify
preserve		perspective
presume		perspire
pretend		persuade
prevail		pertain
prevent		pervade
		pervert

Only a few common words begin with **pur-,** and these words are not often misspelled:

purchase	purpose	purvey

The one occasional troublemaker is **pursue.**

Watch out for these look-alike pairs:

perspective	preserve	permanent	pervert
prospective	persevere	permeate	prevent

Perspire and *perspiration* are spelled *per-*, NOT *pre-*.
A word often needlessly misspelled:

prejudice

This word refers to prejudgment. You can easily recognize the root word, which appears also in *judicial*. The first syllable, *prej-*, sounds as if it ought to be spelled with *dg*, like *hedge*; but it isn't.

counter-, contra- ||||||||||||||||||||||||||||||||||||||||||||||||||||||||||

These prefixes both mean the same thing: opposite to, or against. *Contra-* appears in only a few common words, like *contradict* and *contraceptive*. It has been absorbed into *contrary* and *contrast* and is no longer recognizable as a prefix.

Counter- is by far the more common:

counterinfluence   counteroffer   counterclockwise

ante-, anti- |||||||||||||||||||||||||||||||||||||||||||||||||||||||||||

Ante- means "before": *antecedent* (going before), *anteroom* (a waiting room at the front), *antedate* (to occur earlier in time). The term *ante* in poker is this same word, so used because the *ante* must be placed on the table before cards are dealt.

Anti- means "against." It is easy to remember when the meaning is obvious, as in *antiknock, anticommunist,* and *antiaircraft.* It is a little less obvious in *antibiotic, anticlimax, antidote,* and *antiseptic,* though many people give the *i* in *anti-* a rather strong long *i* sound, and the medical terms suggest the meaning "against."

fore-, for- ||||||||||||||||||||||||||||||||||||||||||||||||||||||||||||

Associate *fore-* with *before* to remember most of the words with the prefix *fore-*. It means "before" in either time or space—earlier, or out in front.

forearm	foregone	foresee
forebear	forehead	foreshadow
forebode	foreman	foreshorten
forecast	foremost	foresight
foreclose	forenoon	foretell
forefather	forerunner	forethought

For- is an Old English prefix long obsolete in the forming of new words. It has several meanings not easy to define, but none overlap with those of **fore-**. In one sense, the prefix is negative, implying separation, exclusion, or loss:

> forbear
> forbid
> forget
> forgive (to give up resentment)
> forgo
> forsake
> forswear

In another sense, **for-** is an intensive, implying something very strongly done:

> forspent   forlorn

The easy way to remember these words is to look for the meaning "before" or "out in front" and use **fore-** for them. Use **for-** for other meanings.

Only two pairs of words overlap:

> forbear   forebear
> forgo   forego

However, knowledge of the meaning of the prefixes will easily prevent your confusing them. **Forbear** means "to refrain or abstain from doing something," as in the phrase "to forbear speaking." **Forebear** is a noun and means "an ancestor"—a "*fore-be-er*," one who has been before. The **-er** ending has shifted to **-ar**, probably by analogy with the word *bear*. **Forgo** means "to give up" or "to do without," as in the phrase "to forgo pleasure." **Forego** means "to go before." It is commonly used as a past participle, **foregone**, as in the phrase "foregone conclusion"; that is, a conclusion already decided in advance, or one that has "gone before."

As usual, there is one illogical exception. The word **forward** has lost the **e**, though this of all words should have kept it. Don't confuse it with **foreword**, the section of a book that comes before the main part.

96· A FINAL WORD OF ADVICE, AND A FINAL TEST

A good speller has learned one simple habit: to see in every word first of all its regular pattern, and then to single out the place in the word (if there is one) that may be irregular. Let's take an example:

upholster

A good speller would not have to pause an instant in putting together the *regular* parts of this word: *"up·ol·ster."* His mind is then free to remember the silent **h.**

If you had to pay conscious attention to every movement of your hands and feet while driving an automobile, you would be a slow, halting, and unconfident driver. The same is true of spelling. The irregularities and exceptions can be easily handled if your mind is free to concentrate on them, rather than on the elementary principles of word-formation.

Let's take another example:

humorous

This word falls into place with the countless words with the **-ous** ending. The first syllable **hu-** is perfectly regular. The middle syllable **-mor-** might cause a doubt as to whether to spell it **-mor-** or *"-mer-."* But since you need not memorize the individual letters of the entire word—everything except the **o** is regular and easy— you can concentrate on that one problem alone and let the rest of the word spell itself. The most irregular words in the English language are really irregular in only a few letters—not all the way through. This is the secret of rapid and accurate spelling: let the regular patterns spell most of the word for you, while you focus on the one or two letters that are exceptional.

Now try your hand at the words below. Where is the difficult spot (if any) in each word? Which letters can you safely remember without effort because they form regular syllables? On which do you need to focus your memory?

428.1
D 76

428, 1
D7C

172 · Downright Irregularities

hoarse	avalanche	aviary
gruesome	vanquish	municipal
biscuit	soliloquy	argument
eager	jewelry	fluorine
speak	dilapidated	verbatim
speech	exorbitant	medieval
view	affidavit	moccasin
aerial	derogatory	piety
superfluous	menagerie	assassin
intravenous	demagogue	traceable
nuisance	dungeon	initiative
poignant	diagnostician	ingredient
innuendo	flagrant	miniature
accessory	demerit	parliament
insipid	vigil	differential
linen	tacit	quotient
denim	material	peculiar
ancient	maniacal	erratic
enervate	esteem	appetite
auxiliary	curiosity	ricochet
prosaic	vineyard	amethyst
carburetor	hiatus	lecherous
trauma	cocoa	jeopardy
essential	punctual	reconnoiter
anxious	huge	repugnant
conscious	wondrous	vagrant
conscience	covet	scandal
fascinate	scoundrel	embarrass
separate	quantity	frightening
amateur	definite	lightning
sleeve	except	familiar
similar	suppress	existence
meant	discoveries	forward
roommate	influential	marriage
safety	optimism	hopeful
colossal	acknowledge	initiate
undoubtedly	embassy	raccoon